Defeat the fox,

Happy birthday Tom

All the best

Moh o Nair.

urban
eden

Adam and James Caplin

For Louis, Noah and Ann

urban eden

Adam and James Caplin

Kyle Cathie Limited

contents

introduction

Last year, James grew enough herbs, fruit, vegetables and salads in his garden to eat something home-grown and totally fresh almost every day during most of spring, summer and autumn. Even in winter there was often something to pick and eat. His garden isn't a vast vegetable plot, nor a kitchen garden. In fact it's a very small but luscious patch of jungle in the heart of the city. It is only 6m (20ft) by 6m (20ft) but there are runner beans twining through jasmine and wisteria, spinach growing beneath roses and great foaming pots of lettuce. James is not a professional gardener, nor is he someone with plenty of time on his hands. He lives a normal, stressed urban existence, with too much to do and too little time to do it.

In another part of the city, on a rooftop high above the traffic, Victoria plum trees thrive amongst tomatoes and nasturtiums. There are cherries and pears, and windowboxes filled with salads. Honeysuckle and viburnum scent the air. For the owner, this rooftop is a sanctuary as well as a source of delicious fresh food and constant beauty. These are Urban Edens. They are small town or city gardens, often surrounded by other gardens and houses, but as close to the Biblical picture of Paradise as you can get in this life.

It makes no sense for an Urban Eden gardener to distinguish plants into ornamental and edible categories. The division may have been useful once, but now it is just restrictive. All it means is that

1

some plants are considered suitable for the domestic garden, while others are deemed appropriate only for the vegetable patch, kitchen garden, or allotment. In reality some edible plants are ornamental and some ornamental plants are edible; some supposedly edible plants are not really worth eating and some supposedly ornamental plants aren't particularly attractive.

The runner bean is a good example. It's a magnificent climber, with superb flowers, elegant fruit and a striking leaf. If the beans weren't edible, more people might grow it in their back gardens! Ironically, it was first introduced into Europe as an ornamental. The Jerusalem artichoke *Helianthus tuberosus* is a relative of the sunflower, with a tall stem and striking yellow flowers; you get the added bonus of its edible tubers. The majestic artichoke *Cynara scolymus* can illuminate an area of border all by itself with its striking powdery green leaves and stunning flowerheads. But because they are thought of as 'edibles' they are all too rarely grown in the ordinary back garden.

Urban Eden gardening isn't, of course, anything new. In many ways, it's a return to an older sort of gardening, going right back to the Biblical idea of a Paradise before the fall. As it says in Genesis: 'Then the Lord God planted a Garden in Eden, in the East, and there he put the man he had formed. He made all kinds of beautiful trees to grow there and produce good fruit.' People only started to divide gardens into edible and ornamental when food became so plentiful that to produce it yourself was a sign of poverty.

Creating a garden like this changes more than just the garden. With edibles growing and being used through the year, the impact of the seasons is felt more strongly and the natural rhythms of life are reinforced. When the sweetcorn seedlings go out, and there are a couple of rainy days, and they start to swell and shoot ahead, the drizzle comes as a positive boon. When the peaches are on the point of ripening, every sunny day has an extra resonance.

Urban Eden gardening is both exciting and satisfying. When something delicious comes from the garden, it's a triumphant feeling. You are, in a powerful and primitive way, making food. You are a provider. Fresh food always tastes better than shop-bought food.

Carrots lose flavour within hours of being picked; salads still juicy from the garden taste deliciously delicate and wonderfully strong at the same time. Lamb cooked with dried rosemary is nowhere near as delicious as lamb cooked with leaves just picked from a bush. The fact that it is your own rosemary, just plucked from the garden, adds to the pleasure.

Seed catalogues offer an extraordinary number of different varieties of vegetables, hundreds more than those typically grown commercially for their qualities of heavy and reliable cropping and long storage. Other varieties offer different advantages, each providing some peculiar delight. You can choose carrots that are short or long, round or tapered, big-rooted, small-rooted, early-cropping, late-cropping, dark orange, light yellow, sweet-tasting, crisp, long-storing, disease-resistant… and so on, and on. The same is true for most vegetables – you only usually see red tomatoes in the shops, but you could grow yellow, orange, white, striped and even black ones, and in many different shapes and sizes.

When you grow your own it also makes you more aware of what is happening in the food chain. Much of

the food we are now sold is either forced indoors, or imported from abroad. You can only wonder what farmers have to do to get their fruit to look perfect and shiny enough for the supermarkets, as home-grown specimens, grown without regular applications of pesticide and fungicide, are nowhere near so perfectly formed, and never shiny.

When you have great-tasting food in the garden, cooking becomes easier. Garden-fresh vegetables are often so delicious that they are best served plain, rather than being 'improved' with sauces and complex recipes. A good crop can help suggest an entire meal. With a superb crop of tiny French beans, the cook thinks about what will be delicious with the beans, rather than treating them as an accompaniment to a main dish. Urban Eden gardening can save you money too. A salad from the garden, followed by a sorrel omelette made, of course, with home-picked sorrel, ending with a couple of your own ripe figs, tastes sublime, and costs hardly anything.

Gardening like this has other profound effects on the Urban Eden gardener. With a constant supply of ever-changing edible plants in the garden, it is tempting to go into the garden even more, if only to check on what is ready to pick and eat. Looking closely at plants, regularly, brings to the attention all the other creatures that live in and amongst the plants, creatures that are all too often ignored. This includes birds and insects, slugs and snails. These creatures have a vital part to play and fascinating lives and habits. Once you get interested in them, they become less unnecessary pests or thieves than things with their own mysterious beauty. Adam and Eve, after all, shared the Garden of Eden with all animal life.

Becoming aware of insect life and eating your own produce means it makes sense to be careful about what is sprayed on the garden. The less you spray, the more creatures will make their home there and eventually the balance will often tip against the pests, making it easier to maintain your garden without chemicals. An Urban Eden should hum with life, morning, noon and night.

Ornamental plants are vital in any Urban Eden. Their beauty is, in itself, a form of nourishment, vital for many of us whose environment during the day is predominantly one of paper, glass, plastic and concrete. There is no need to deprive yourself of delights such as the white jodhpurs on the *Dicentra spectabilis* 'Alba' in spring, the chalky-pink flowers of *Geranium* 'Russell Pritchard' throughout summer, the fluorescent blue flowers of *Ceratostigma willmottianum* in autumn, or the incomparable scent of a *Daphne odora* 'Aureomarginata' in winter. Flowers also help attract numerous insects such as hoverflies, whose larvae eat aphids, helping to protect Urban Edens from pests.

It is partly because of the interplay of all these elements that this way of gardening doesn't have to be time-consuming. Designed in the right way, an Urban Eden can thrive perfectly well if you don't have much time for it, and do better if you have more time for regular care. Urban Eden gardening can also be quite a social activity. When there is a glut – even three runner bean plants, at the height of the season, can produce beans by the bagful – these can be shared with friends and neighbours. In return, you will probably receive something they have grown or cooked. Such exchange brings rewards of its own, reinforcing the sense of

community that is such a vital part of urban life.

A luscious garden in full swing is a delight for children. When they can go into the garden and pick their own fresh strawberries, even if there aren't many of them, it fires up an interest in plants, an appreciation which can be invaluable for an urban child. There are all sorts of wonderful lessons, from basic ones like the difference between ripe and unripe colours to the pleasure of nurturing, the miracle of planting their first seeds and having plants grow from them. Children love the process of picking food, and having it appear later on the table, transformed by cooking into something that they love to eat. The Urban Eden can be a place of magic for them.

But you don't even have to have a garden to grow something delicious in the middle of a city, as long as you have some access to the open air. When James lived in a flat with only a balcony, he grew a big pot of new potatoes, and one glorious summer evening when entertaining some friends, tipped out the pot, scrubbed off the potatoes and ate them there and then with butter and fresh garlic. Paradise, in the middle of the city.

There isn't a single, ideal Urban Eden. It is an approach rather than a prescription. You can add a few elements of our ideas to your existing garden, or plunge in and do it wholesale. Adam, a professional gardener who designs small gardens and has a well-established wild garden in the urban heartland, was initially sceptical that you could grow anything much worth eating in a garden of only 6m (20ft) by 6m (20ft). Once he saw James's garden in action, fruit, herbs and vegetables began appearing in his wilderness.

Welcome to the Urban Eden!

2

healthy gardens

Many people who live in towns assume that it would not be advisable to eat anything grown in their garden because the air is too polluted, or the soil too contaminated. In fact, vegetables, herbs, salads and fruit grown in almost all gardens in the town or city are just as delicious and healthy as those grown in the country.

Lead, a prime pollution suspect, is present as tiny particles in the exhaust of vehicles that run on leaded petrol. As these particulates are heavier than air, they only travel at a low level between 20 and 50m (70 and 165ft) across open ground. So the problem posed by the lead in exhausts is relatively local. Only a very small number of gardens in very specific locations have a pollution problem. These are located on or near old industrial sites like tanneries, gasworks or asphalt factories. But even in these unfortunate gardens, there are ways of growing herbs, vegetables and even fruit successfully and safely.

On the other hand, most soil in the city – unless it has been loved and nurtured by a keen gardener – needs a boost before plants will really thrive in it. The old gardening cliché is true: 'The answer's in the soil.' If the soil is well drained, full of organic matter, containing plenty of nutrients, it is astonishing how well almost every plant will grow in it. Improving soil is one of the simplest and most rewarding things anyone can do in the garden.

Lead

For gardeners the concern comes from main roads with their constant stream of cars, often stuck in traffic jams, spewing out exhaust fumes night and day. But if your garden is more than 50m (165ft) from a busy road, you need not worry about lead from vehicle exhausts polluting your soil. Moreover, if there is a house between the main road and the garden, that is a further barrier. Happily, as lead in petrol is being phased out, any problem is lessening. So lead pollution from vehicle exhausts should not a problem for most urban gardens.

Even with gardens close to busy roads, soil tests rarely uncover dangerous levels of lead. However, it is always better to be safe than sorry so if you want to grow edibles in these situations the best advice is to add large quantities of compost and manure to the land.

This has a dual effect. First, it dilutes any lead that may be in the soil by adding bulky, clean matter. Second, it changes the soil chemistry so as to reduce the take-up of any lead by plants. If in doubt, owners of roadside gardens should get the soil tested for lead contamination by the appropriate local environmental department.

If you are unfortunate enough to have a garden where there is a problem, or if you are worried about it in spite of the evidence, you can still grow wonderful edible plants in bought-in soil in containers or raised beds (see pages 19).

Industry

The soil on sites that have been used for industry (gasworks, asbestos works, kilns, ceramic, cement and asphalt manufacturing sites etc.) is often polluted with chemicals that persist in the ground for a long time and can be taken up by plants. Unfortunately, areas close to these sites may have contaminated soil, as toxic chemicals may have been carried there by groundwater. Also, tall industrial chimneys spread pollutants a long way downwind of old industries, and, no matter how clean these industries may be now, in the recent past the situation may have been very different.

If your garden is near one of these old industrial sites, be cautious. Check with the environmental department, who generally have maps showing brown-field sites, and may even test your soil if there are real concerns. If you know, or are told, that your soil is unsuitable for growing food plants, but you still want to enjoy home-grown produce, there's nothing to stop you growing edible plants in containers (see below) using soil you know to be clean. This can be a mixture of bought-in and home-composted (see page 27) material. With a bit of planning, you can soon fill a lot of containers and grow a delightful range of edibles in an otherwise ornamental garden. But in this situation you need to be alert to the risk posed by soil splash. Wash everything thoroughly before eating it.

New developments The soil is often of questionable quality in new developments where the garden topsoil has been imported. In the past, developers may occasionally have used soil from less than ideal sources, although increasingly tough legislation and heightened awareness about environmental pollution make this a rare occurrence today. But if you are worried, check with the developer. However, in nearly all new developments you will have to improve the soil greatly (see pages 20–31).

Containers

Containers are extremely useful in any Urban Eden, whatever the soil condition. They mean you can grow much more in a small garden: hanging baskets can be filled with tumbling tomatoes or strawberries and hung in the sun; a courgette can be put halfway up a wall in a hay basket; a peach tree can sit in a container on a patio or balcony. You can create brilliant visual displays simply by massing containers together. You can also place containers together to make lovely, surprising combinations, even though flowering and fruiting tomatoes and beans, for example, may have got to this stage growing in different parts of the garden.

Right Urban environments are full of unexpected places to grow fruiting plants, herbs, salads and vegetables. This house has a side entrance with a door on to a quiet road beyond and the space provides a sheltered spot for growing edibles. The owners pass through here many times a day, throughout the year, so get constant pleasure from the plants, which receive plenty of attention. If the road had been busier, or the site more exposed, edibles could have been grown here in containers. Most city back gardens are also safe for growing food plants as the houses provide an effective barrier from most airborne lead particles.

However, it is more work growing in containers than just leaving plants in the earth. For a start, they have a limited water-holding capacity and so need regular watering. Holidays can be a problem. Go away in the summer for two weeks, and you could return to find all the plants in pots dead. There are various commercial reservoirs that will supply some water, though with a sizeable collection of pots this can be expensive. The best solution, if you are going away and cannot ask a friend or neighbour to water, is to put the plants in the deepest shade available, and to give them a very thorough soaking. Any mulching that can be added around the plants will help.

Style Nowadays, containers come in a wide variety of materials. These include plain terracotta, glazed terracotta, coloured terracotta, plastic that looks like terracotta, plastic that looks like plastic, wood (barrels, windowboxes), ceramics, metal and so on. In fact, anything that can contain soil can be made into a container: old baths and sinks are favourites, as are chimney pots, buckets and large food tubs. Whatever you use, it must have drainage holes or plants may drown.

There are certain places where the choice of pot needs to be governed by more than aesthetics. Where load-bearing is a concern, as on many balconies and roofs, plastic is usually recommended because it is light. Set against this is the disadvantage that a light pot containing a big plant can easily be blown over. Sometimes the only solution to this is to use a light pot, and to tie the plant to something solid in order to keep it upright in heavy wind. On a roof, put the heaviest pots round the edges, and if possible near the corners. On a balcony, if weight is a concern, put the pots near the wall of the building.

Size When growing in containers, you should always try to put the plant in an appropriate-size pot. A small plant in too large a pot will rarely thrive. However, too small a pot will get dry very quickly, requiring constant watering. When you plant up a large container, it is a good idea to sink a small empty plastic bottle, with small holes punched in the bottom, into the soil, with its top protruding slightly above the top of the soil. Filling this with water will help keep the soil in the container moist for a longer period.

Don't be afraid of using an eclectic mix of containers. Stylised metal containers, traditional terracotta pots and the cut-off bottoms of plastic bottles can work extremely well together.
Below left Grow a mix of basil plants on a sunny windowsill. Individually they look great, but they are even better as a collection.
Below centre One of the advantages of using a plastic bottle as a container is that it is light and robust.
Below right A view of the garden from the kitchen window provides extra inspiration for the cook and added perspective to the view. There will also be gorgeous scents in summer when the window is open.

Left and above **Raised beds are excellent in small gardens. They are a great way of growing a lot of plants as the soil used in the bed can be imported and kept in tiptop condition, able to support a very intensive planting. Raised beds have other advantages too for the Urban Eden gardener. Being built up above ground level, they are easy to tend. Trailing fruit and vegetables can be grown on the edge so that they tumble over the sides, adding an extra visual element, and keeping the produce clear of the soil. The whole bed, and its raised planting, instantly adds height to an otherwise flat area of garden.**

Raised beds

In many new developments – and in neglected older gardens – there is little if any topsoil. One way of transforming a garden like this is to build slightly raised beds. These need only be about 15cm (6in) high. They work best where the garden boundary is a stone or brick wall as raised soil will eventually rot a fence. Be careful about banking soil up against house walls because any damp course must not be breached.

Build up the front of the bed with old railway sleepers, or bricks, or even crazy paving on edge. Dig over the existing surface of the bed, then simply fill the space with rich compost or manure and topsoil.

The front of a fairly low raised bed is ideal for tumbling plants like strawberries. The edge creates a bold visual line, which can be emphasised with a border planting of mixed herbs, perhaps interspersed with nasturtiums and alyssum. Because the bed is raised, the topsoil will drain well. Every autumn for the first few years a new raised bed will need to be topped up with fresh soil as everything settles and the organic matter filters down to the lower levels.

Below Bought-in compost is of guaranteed quality and is ideal for containers, being neither too sticky nor too friable. Sticky soils tend to get waterlogged which will damage many plants, while water tends to pass too quickly through soils which are too gritty, leaching out the nutrients.

Improving the soil – starting points

The soil in urban gardens is often tired and lifeless. In these gardens hardly any weeds grow in spite of there being bare earth; the surface of the bed during wet weather may be tinged green with a slimy growth; the earth cracks in drought; and when it is turned over the soil is dense, compact and is host to few if any worms. Growing anything well in soils like this will be a struggle. Virtually any soil, whatever it is like, will benefit from having more organic matter added to it. But

the fine-tuning of how to improve a soil depends on what you are starting with.

Real soil experts look hard at a new soil, roll it in their fingers and sniff it. We've even seen one soil consultant pop a bit in his mouth and grind it in his teeth to establish its exact nature. This might have told him things the other tests did not; on the other hand, it may have been part of an elaborate charade to convince others of his expertise! Whatever, most of us need only look carefully at the soil and rub a bit between our fingers. If it is dark-coloured, feels sticky and rolls into balls it is a clay soil. If it is gritty and falls apart it is sandy. If it is smooth and silky, it is silt. If it is dry and crumbly, and looks grey, it contains chalk. All benefit from adding copious organic matter, but each requires other things too.

Drainage Soil doesn't just provide plants with nutrients, it is also the means by which they obtain water. The best soil holds water well in summer, and drains well in winter. Badly drained soils (clay and silt) get wet and cold and stay that way for a long time. It can be hard work to improve their drainage: you need to add lots of horticultural grit or gravel to the sub-soil, and possibly even consider soakaways and land drains. If a bed is empty, or you are starting one afresh, you could double dig it. Remove the topsoil in one strip, putting it to one side (in bags is a good idea in cramped urban gardens). Then work organic matter into the subsoil. Now fill the trench with soil from the strip of land beside the trench, exposing the next strip of subsoil. Add organic matter to that and move along the bed till you reach the end, where you finally get to use the topsoil from the first trench.

Or you could build a raised bed straight onto the soil or even subsoil and fill it with topsoil containing plenty of well-rotted manure. Hungry plants like beans, asparagus and squashes will love these conditions and will thrive without constant fertilising and watering. But if you want to grow plants that dislike wet feet, such as Mediterranean herbs like thymes, rosemary and oregano, grow them in containers.

DIFFERENT SOILS AND THEIR PROPERTIES

Sand Water rushes right through sandy soils, leaching out nutrients and organic matter. To improve such soil, put lots of rich organic matter which contains plenty of nutrients on the surface, digging it in only lightly. It will quickly be carried down (much too quickly, in fact). This needs to be done regularly. Mulch in spring to reduce the problem of drying out. Tarragon, thyme and rosemary will taste very strong when grown in these conditions, but greedier plants such as peas and beans will not thrive in them.

Clay This is full of plant nutrients, but drains badly in winter, and bakes hard in summer. The trick is to catch the soil when it is neither too wet, nor too dry, and dig plenty of organic matter and coarse grit into it. If possible leave it open in winter for the frost to break it apart further.

Chalk These soils contain little organic matter because they are made of relatively big particles, and are often stony. They drain well, sometimes too freely. The best treatment is to dig organic matter and mulches into the top surface during the growing season. Rotted grass-cuttings (which are acid) and moss peat are also good as they counteract the alkalinity of the chalk. The soil will probably swallow up vast quantities without much visible difference. However, done regularly, it really is worth it.

Silts While silts are fertile and retain water well, they can get waterlogged. Improve the soil when it is reasonably dry, adding coarse grit and lots of well-rotted compost.

Peat Peaty soils are generally good but can be rather short on nutrients. Keep them well fed with compost or liquid feed.

Organic matter Ironically, there is a downside to growing healthy plants that crop well: they take a lot out of the soil. If the leaves and fruit those plants produce are eaten (rather than permitted to fall onto the soil and, by rotting, return to it) the soil is going to get poorer and poorer, year on year. So the soil must be replenished regularly.

Organic matter or humus comes in many forms: animal manures, spent mushroom compost, spent hops, composts made of seaweed, composted green waste, peat and home-made compost. The simplest way to add it to the soil is to put a layer of it on the surface of your beds every autumn. Use 8–10cm (3–4in) of home-made compost, slightly less of spent mushroom compost or hops, and only a fairly thin layer of the stronger manures. This should be taken down into the soil during winter by rain and earthworms. Any remaining on the surface in the spring should be forked in lightly. On clay soils, if you dig the humus in lightly in the autumn this makes it available to plants much more quickly. But if you are the sort of gardener who really wants a productive patch, add well-rotted organic matter throughout the season. It is a wonderful mulch in hot weather.

Different soil improvers – composts and manure

Coir The outer, hairy covering of coconuts can be used as a soil conditioner which helps open up heavy soils. It contains virtually no nutrients, so the soil also needs to be fed to keep it in top condition.

Bark Another waste product, bark is a wonderful mulch. But it should not be dug in as it will consume the nitrogen in the soil as it rots.

Peat Peat is light, widely available and very convenient but, sadly, it is relatively ineffective because rain quickly washes peat through the soil, which means it has to be added year after year. This makes it an expensive option. It is

Right Kitchen and garden waste will break down into crumbly dark compost which is a perfect general soil improver and conditioner.
Below right Well-rotted manure has almost no smell and is easy to work with. You can mix it with other compost and apply generously around fruit and vegetable beds, incorporating it into the soil or leaving it on top as a mulch in autumn or winter. Or you can apply it more sparingly on its own. Some greedy vegetables, such as squashes and potatoes, adore muck, while Mediterranean herbs hate it. Don't put fresh manure straight onto your garden as it is too harsh for most plants and tends to burn their foliage.

Above **Mushroom compost is light and crumbly, pleasant to work with and easy to get hold of. It is suitable for most plants except those that prefer an acid soil. As an extra bonus you may even get an occasional crop of edible mushrooms.**

environmentally suspect as peat mining is destroying the bogs around the world from which it is extracted.

Spent mushroom compost Mushrooms are grown on a mixture of animal manure, something that holds water (like peat) and chalk. Once the mushrooms have been harvested, this spent compost is removed to be replaced by a fresh, sterile mix. This spent compost is a wonderful soil conditioner. It is high in nutrients, has a great water-holding capacity and is very pleasant to work with. The only drawback is that it is slightly alkali, so does not suit acid-loving plants like rhododendrons, camellias and blueberries.

Seaweed meal Seaweed, washed of salt, has long been used by farming communities with access to the sea to improve the quality of their soil. Seaweed meal, which is dried and ground seaweed, is particularly rich in trace elements, and improves soil structure.

Municipal compost As more and more people are turning to recycling, local authorities are increasingly setting up schemes to compost green waste from gardens. This is sometimes available for free, but is more often only delivered by the lorry load. Since many different gardens contribute their waste to this compost, some of them will have been spraying with all sorts of chemicals. Although the heat of a big compost heap will kill most weed seeds and pathogens, it won't degrade these chemical residues so the quality cannot be guaranteed.

Manure Most plants, apart from herbs and wildflowers, love a bit of manure, as it contains all the trace elements that plants need to thrive. It breaks down slowly in the soil, giving plants a boost throughout the growing season. For the Urban Eden gardener, adding manure to the garden is deeply satisfying. Before cynics scoff that manure is not available in towns and cities, garden centres increasingly sell bags of various types and athough it may appear expensive, a little goes a long way in a small garden, and does a great deal of good.

You may even be able to collect your own horse manure from small commercial stables for hobby riders, or from police stables near the centre of towns. There are also a number of urban farms in towns and cities. All are great sources of muck, and the people running them are usually only too willing to let gardeners take a bit if you supply your own bags and take a shovel. The best manure for the garden is mixed with straw rather than with wood-shavings which can introduce disease into your garden, and will attract a plague of wood lice.

Fresh manure is too strong for immediate use and can

Below Peat-based composts are widely available and suitable for most planting requirements. They are very light which is convenient for packing and storage but means they must be thoroughly soaked when planting, and they don't hold nutrients for long. Environmentalists advise choosing a substitute such as coir.

chemically burn plants. The best way to deal with it is to add it to the compost bin (see page 29) in layers about 8–10cm (3–4in) deep, putting 15cm (6in) of other compost material between each layer of manure. Keep the excess in the bags in which it was collected, tied up with string to stop the rain getting in, hidden somewhere inconspicuous. After some time the bag may smell a bit, but the manure will keep. When the compost bin is restarted, you will then have a bit of manure to add to the new compost to speed up its development.

Soil-based versus soil-less composts

Composts can broadly be divided into those that are soil-based, and those that are soil-less. While either are suitable for adding to ground-level beds, each suits different kinds of container planting.

Soil-based composts The main constituent of soil-based composts is topsoil. This is a good source of nutrients over the long term, and holds both added nutrients and water well. So these composts are good for more permanent plantings, such as small fruit trees and herbs. They are also heavy, so ideal where a plant is exposed to wind and needs anchoring. But that weight can also be a disadvantage where load-bearing is an issue – on most balconies and roofs. Another disadvantage is that quality can be variable, depending on the source of topsoil. Their water-retaining properties can also

cause a problem, as heavy rain or over watering can increase the weight of soil-based composts dramatically. With less than perfect drainage, they can also become sticky. To avoid this, always put lots of crocks in the bottom of pots.

Soil-less composts These are usually peat-based, but see if you can find those with different bases (see page 22–3). These composts are best for growing annuals. They are light, and easy to handle, and since most commercially grown plants start life in peat-based composts, they root freely when transplanted into them. There are multipurpose soil-less composts that suit plants of all ages. Once a peat-based compost gets dry, it needs a thorough drenching, or to be plunged in water till the compost gets wet again.

The fact that soil-less composts are light is a drawback where wind is a problem. Another disadvantage is that they rely on added fertilisers for their goodness. As a result, plants in soil-less composts will require feeding sooner than plants in soil-based composts. Some soil-less composts also contain imidacloprid to combat vine weevils and aphids, and although this may be very convenient for ornamental plantings imidacloprid has yet to be tested for its effect on humans, so these composts are not recommended for edibles.

Ericaceous composts should be used for plants that require an acid soil, like blueberries and rhododendrons.

Home-made compost

Home-made compost is totally in tune with the Urban Eden philosophy. It is free, environmentally friendly, and is more effective at improving soil over the long term than many proprietary composts. There are many ways to compost and people can become incredibly passionate and combative about it.

Making your own compost is one of those astonishing natural processes that gives great pleasure. It begins with a pile of old leaves, thrown-away scraps and flowers, and ends up with crumbly compost. Composted organic matter will

inoculate the soil with a whole range of tiny organisms – micro-fauna – some of which will help your plants to resist attack from pests and diseases and will also help them take up more nutrients.

The environmental benefits are greatest if kitchen waste is used as one of the ingredients of compost, simultaneously improving your soil and reducing the amount that is thrown away into landfill sites. It is the ultimate recycling: plant makes food, food makes compost, compost helps make plant.

The traditional way is to make a compost heap, but few small urban gardens have the space, so a compost bin is a good solution.

Compost bins

Commercially produced compost bins are excellent for the slightly larger garden. For the smaller garden, an ordinary plastic dustbin with a lid will do. Pierce the dustbin with holes approximately 1 cm (1.2in) in diameter all round and in the bottom to let liquids drain out.

The problem in most small gardens is where to put the bin. The best solution is to hide it in an area for storing tools. A small bin can also be incorporated into a group of pot plants, or hidden behind a dense evergreen plant. Never place it near a pond as the run-off is quite acidic and can kill the fish.

To begin To start the process of composting, simply put all garden clippings in the bin, together with any fruit and vegetable that goes off, all vegetable peelings, and old cut flowers. Continue to add garden clippings, old fruit and vegetable peelings, and after a while (the length of time depends on the bin, what's in it, and the weather), it will all be converted into crumbly brown compost with an earthy smell.

Never add left-over cooked fish or meat as it will smell as it goes off and will attract rats and other vermin. Don't add any part of any vegetable or plant that looks diseased, as the disease might spread through the compost, and from there into your soil where it could infect other plants of the same food type that are grown later. Also, avoid putting weeds that are covered with seeds into this sort of compost bin. In a traditional heap which is fairly big and is built mainly in autumn, the heat rises high enough to kill weed seeds. In a small compost bin, that doesn't happen and weed seeds will survive and be spread with the compost.

Try to build up your compost in layers of different material each about 15cm (6in) deep. Make sure the compost is always covered, otherwise the rain will get in and the whole thing will become a soggy, smelly mess. At first, the greenery will just sit there, and the level inside the bin will rise inexorably. Then, after perhaps six months, it will begin to fall as the composting process gets going in earnest.

Left **You can make a compost bin by drilling holes in the sides and base of a galvanised dustbin. It can nestle in an inconspicuous corner of the garden, but it is most convenient if it is not too far from the kitchen, so that adding your scraps to it is easy and becomes routine.**
Above **Composting vegetable waste from the kitchen is the ultimate recycling: using the remains of food to grow more food.**

Once under way When the bin is about three quarters full, stop adding new material. Instead, put the new material into a heavy-duty bag, which can be stored inside the bin. This will be the start of your next compost. After another couple of months, turn out the bin. In addition to the soggy rotten vegetable matter in the bag, there should be a pile of dark, earthy-smelling matter, which will contain a few uncomposted things like twigs and a few stubborn things that have tried sprouting. To restart the process, line the bottom of the bin with fresh greenery, and tip the mushy mess from the bag onto it. If enough is available, cover this with more greenery.

To improve quality During the process it's a great help to turn the compost at least once. This introduces air into the material, and mixes very-well-composted and not-so-well-composted material. Simply get all the half-composted stuff out of the bin and shovel it all back in, mixing layers as you go. The result is a better-rotted, more even compost. In a larger garden where you have a lot of clippings and prunings, a shredder is a great help to composting. Shredded leaves compost startlingly quickly because microbes can get into all the cut areas immediately. A compost bin with minced leaves will also heat up more than a normal one, producing a finer, cleaner compost.

Worm bins

If you have not got room for any sort of compost bin, a worm bin is a superb alternative. Most gardens, even those with compost heaps, would benefit from a worm bin. Increasingly, ready-to-use worm bins with a starter pack of worms are available in shops. Also, many mail-order organic gardening companies sell worms and worm bins. The best ones have a tap at the bottom to take off the liquid manure the worms produce.

Worms will turn almost all kitchen waste into a superb, strong compost. This includes tea-bags, coffee grounds, stale

Right One of the incidental pleasures of gardening is to get close to the creatures in your garden. Worms are gardeners' best friends, breaking down and spreading organic matter in the garden. The more worms there are in your compost, the more there will be in your soil, distributing food, helping drainage, aeration and general fertility. The more there are in your soil, the healthier it will be.

breadcrumbs and fruit and vegetable peelings (but not potato peelings or garlic). The dark, spongy compost they produce is very high in nutrients, as is the liquid that is tapped off from the bin. This liquid is so strong it should be used diluted by 10 to 1. The worms are also fascinating creatures, and wormery owners often get quite passionate about them!

Adding compost When the compost is ready, pick out the uncomposted twigs and sticks, and spread the rest on the earth. You can leave it on top of the soil or dig it in. If it is left on top, the compost acts as a mulch until the worms drag it under and of decomposition reduces it completely. It looks excellent too, because the surface of the beds is a pleasing dark brown. Set against that, digging in the compost speeds up the rate at which plants can benefit from its nutrients and immediately improves the soil's water-holding capacity.

Microclimates

In even a small Urban Eden there can be a huge range of conditions, some of which can be quite extreme. There may be a big wall on one side of the garden, which plunges a whole bed into shadow. That bed will be comparatively cold, damp and shady. On the other side of the garden there may be a corner of a bed that is sunny for most of the day in summer. That corner can become blisteringly hot.

Suitable plants To garden effectively and happily in these conditions you need to pick plants which enjoy them. The cool, damp bed can play host to a massed planting of spinach *Spinacia oleracea*, with wild strawberries *Fragaria vesca semperflorens* fruiting and flowering on the edges, and sorrel *Rumex acetosa* in clumps. Even lettuce will enjoy these conditions. A climber like a bean may be able to rise above the shade and find some sun.

In the hot corner, herbs like thyme and tarragon will thrive, as will a peach, or grape vine, or even quite exotic-looking plants like a Cape gooseberry *Physalis species* with its delicious orange fruit encased in papery chinese lanterns. If the summer heat is too intense, a pergola or tree will provide the shade necessary to protect plants in the height of summer.

Rain Also note the way rain hits a garden. Buildings and walls cast rain shadows and the soil for about 30cm (12in) or so at the base of a straight wall doesn't get as wet as the soil in the main part of the bed. This shadow is larger if the wall is very high, or there are overhanging eaves or balconies. That is why it is good practice, when planting a tree against a wall, to put its root ball at least 30cm (12in) out into the bed, with its trunk leaning in. Check constantly that plants trained against the wall are not dry, even after a period of rain.

Wind An Urban Eden surrounded by walls can be very sheltered. Many plants love this (French beans, sweetcorn, cucumbers) but a few do not. Gooseberries, for instance, suffer from mildew when the air is still. Balconies are at the other extreme as they are often windy, especially on a long straight street which can funnel the wind. Weighting pots down with a mulch of gravel or big pebbles is one way to help with anchoring the pot, and retaining water in the soil. It is a good practice to place small pots in the shelter of larger ones.

The easiest way to work out what can be grown is to look around to see what other people with similar gardens are growing. If they have an olive, you can have an olive. But you need to bear in mind that just because there is an olive tree in their garden doesn't mean that they produce enough fruit to make their own virgin oil every year! Plants fruit in a much smaller range of locations than they are able to survive in. But don't get too concerned that all your plants should be productive: there is a place for every beautiful plant in an Urban Eden. If it gives you pleasure, grow it.

3

Windowsills · Salad pots · Containers · Fruit in containers · Balconies · Roof gardens ·
Edible borders · Fruit trees · Walls · Ground cover

what to grow...

Many edible plants are extremely easy to grow. You just pop seed in the ground, keep the plant watered, protect it a bit, and hey presto: food. After all, people have grown plants and eaten them for many thousands of years without any of the modern conveniences we nowadays take for granted – piped water, soil improvers, mass-produced tools, gardening manuals and suchlike. When you first venture into growing food plants, stick to those that are robust, tolerant, ready-cropping and good-looking, then you'll find Urban Eden gardening easy and fulfilling.

There are a few tricky vegetables. As a boy, Adam tried to grow a soya bean *Glycine max*, the photograph on the seed packet inspiring visions of an abundant harvest. The plant just managed to limp into existence, and produced one single bean that didn't ripen. He felt a complete failure, and didn't attempt to grow anything edible for years.

Also, for some mysterious reason, even experienced gardeners can't grow everything. We know an expert who fails with basil, James cannot grow radishes, and Adam has trouble with thyme. The moral is: if something doesn't work, don't worry, try something else. Experimenting is fun, and surprisingly exciting as you don't know exactly what the new plant will do next, and when it works, you get something delicious to eat, and a whole new range of plants to play with next season.

Windowsills

A windowsill is a superb place to start growing edible plants. All you need are a few pots or a windowbox and a little good soil, and to water and feed the plants occasionally – you don't even need to bend to pick the crop. The best plants are those that produce constantly and tend to stay small.

Sunny sills For a sunny spot, a good first choice is thyme *Thymus vulgaris* or pot marjoram *Origanum onites*. Both are perennial herbs that don't mind limited soil and thrive in the heat and moderate neglect. Plant them in soil-based compost with good drainage, water them regularly but not too much and allow the soil to dry out between waterings, which for most of us is something that comes naturally. You will be able to pick fresh herbs for most of the year, enjoy the flowers in summer and the aroma of warm Mediterranean hills coming from their foliage on sunny evenings. After years of failure, Adam has now taken all the thyme from his borders and is at last growing it successfully in pots. Pot-grown herbs also tend to taste more intense than those grown in a well-watered garden with rich deep soil.

Bay *Laurus nobilis* does well on a sill, even in a small pot. It seems to match its rate of growth to the available root space, growing slowly in a small pot, and vigorously in open ground. The soil in a pot growing bay will need refreshing every couple of years, and after a while the plant may begin to pine for more space, at which point you will need to transfer it to a bigger pot, or put it in the ground. But while it is on the sill its dark-green, finely shaped leaves and small white flowers are highly attractive and the smell of a bay tree warmed by the sun is very evocative; fresh bay enlivens all sorts of dishes. A potted bay also responds well to being standardised and turned into a sculptural mini-ball on a stem.

Basil *Ocimum basilicum* is another classic herb for a windowsill. The smaller-leafed varieties, such as bush basil *Ocimum basilicum* var. *minimum,* are particularly easy to grow and make very attractive and compact bushes with soft green

Below Indoor and outdoor windowsills are ideal for herbs and small vegetables, and plants such as chives and perpetual spinach will grow happily in shade or part shade.
Right French lavender *Lavandula stoechas* is beautiful, strongly perfumed and an ideal companion for many vegetables as it attracts beneficial insects and helps repel pests.

Below **Sun-loving vegetables such as chillies will flourish outside in even cooler temperate climates if you move them into the sunniest spots in the garden to give them the best chance. Turn plants regularly so that the sun gets to every part of them and all the fruits ripen.**

leaves that almost always manage to look healthy. Tarragon *Artemisia dracunculus* is a wonderful culinary herb, and quite hard to grow in an open bed where the water that other plants require can depress it to the point of death. It can thrive, however, in a pot placed in direct sun and given water in moderation. Tarragon dies back in winter and is not entirely hardy, like another herb that will love a sunny sill but needs protection in winter, lemon grass *Cymbopogon cytratus*. Pot it into good, rich soil, and be careful not to overwater. If possible, shelter your tarragon and lemon grass somewhere cool and dry over winter and they will resprout the following year.

A planting of mixed lettuces is surprisingly attractive (see page 38), and French beans, sweet or chilli peppers and chard get a head start in pots and windowboxes on larger windowsills. Sow them indoors in spring and plant outside in a larger pot or windowbox in a sheltered site when they are large enough to handle. They are all attractive plants and provide lots of interest (beans and peppers produce flowers and fruit over quite a long period) as well as fresh food. There is something magical about reaching out of the window, plucking a handful of beans, popping them into boiling water and eating them no more than five minutes later.

Strawberries are good in pots and windowboxes. Their daisy-like flowers are pretty and the fruit ripens well when hanging over the edge of the pot. But strawberries are hungry feeders, and require regular feeding and plenty of water if you are to get even a few decent berries regularly.

A collection of edibles in pots on a windowsill looks inviting and refreshing with their different-shaped leaves and different-coloured greens – as attractive as any ornamentals. Herbs thrive better in pots than in mixed plantings in a windowbox as you can tailor the conditions to each herb's preference.

Shady sills You can grow a good range of edibles on even a shady windowsill, as long as the shade is not too deep. Chives thrive in these conditions; although they like the sun, they are tolerant of shade, and it is always useful to have a handful of fresh chives to hand. Simply put the plants in good soil, water them often and clip them regularly. You can leave them there all year for future years' cropping, or plant them in the garden when they die back and replenish the sill with winter salad leaves or ornamentals.

Sorrel *Rumex acetosa* is happy on shady sills, and makes marvellous piquant sauces. Grow from seed and when plants are established pot into a fairly large container of about 20cm (8in) of rich soil. The smaller-leafed *Rumex scutatus* is perhaps more ornamental, and excellent in salads. It is low-growing, and prefers a peat-based compost. Cut sorrel's flowers to

Plant selection When planting a mixed selection in a windowbox, only combine plants that like the same conditions. Dwarf French beans like good soil and plenty of moisture, so grow beautifully with French marigolds and curly parsley. Pick the French beans as soon as they are big enough to eat and deadhead the marigolds to ensure continuous fruiting and flowering for many weeks, even months if given liquid feed regularly. Thyme would be unhappy in this planting because it does not appreciate much water, and would be overwhelmed by the other plants. A small lettuce however, like Black Seeded Simpson, would be a good substitute for curly parsley, as it would appreciate the moist fertile soil, and grows well enough to hold its own.

Planting method Another way to use a windowbox is to half sink pots containing herbs into it, ensuring you can get the watering regime just right and you can turn the pots from time to time to give the herbs sun all around. If you place a more vigorous flowering plant in the box under the pots to trail down, you get a very attractive and lush effect. Three pots of thyme, alternating the silvery green foliage of *Thymus* 'Silver Queen' with the dark leaves of *Thymus vulgaris*, rising out of a sea of red and white flowering trailing geranium would make a stunning display on a sunny sill, and would give pleasure all summer long.

Identical planting A row of identical plants in pots also makes an attractive windowsill display. A regiment of basil looks particularly effective and is very practical as the fresh leaves are so delicious that it is tempting to eat them all the time; with a selection of pots you can crop each one hard in turn.

Above **Harvesting sorrel as part of a salad for one.**
Right **An old sink makes an excellent container for an attractive mixed salad crop, here ready for the first picking.**

encourage a better crop of leaves. Perpetual spinach *Beta vulgaris cycla*, and Swiss chard *Beta vulgaris* are also happy in shade, and their generous spear-shaped leaves look quite magnificent in a windowbox.

As long as a windowsill is not too exposed, a trailing cucumber *Cucumis sativus* will be happy and very decorative on a shady sill. A cucumber needs a fairly big pot, at least 20cm (8in), plenty of water when flowers are developing and high potash feed when fruiting. Cucumbers will form very regularly, and grow to a good size with indecent haste. You could train the cucumber vines to climb round your sill, and enjoy a striking view and a summer of fresh cucumbers.

Salad pots

A partially shaded sill is an ideal place to grow a windowbox of salad, or a large salad pot, stunning wherever you grow it. You need a pot at least 20cm (8in) diameter, fill it with compost (lettuce is not fussy, either soil-less, or soil-based, or a mix will do) and sprinkle seeds of a cut-and-come-again salad mix on it. Sow seeds from mid-spring till the end of autumn to provide lettuce most of the year round. Suitable salad mixes are sometimes described by seed companies as loose-leafed lettuce; the most attractive mixtures include frilly leafed varieties such as Lolla Rossa and Lollo Biondi and those with crumpled leaves such as Black Seeded Simpson. Ten seeds will be more than enough spread evenly in one pot, so reseal your seed packet and store it somewhere cool and dry for later. To ensure a continuous supply of lettuces, plant two salad pots, sowing the seed of the second one month after the first.

Lettuce seeds germinate quickly, and the little plants burst into leaf very enthusiastically. Within a couple of weeks there will be a group of lettuce seedlings in the pot. Within six or seven weeks the pot should be an exuberant froth of lettuces jostling for room. In early summer it takes only about 40 days for the lettuces to grow to maturity, longer in autumn. So, when you want a salad, or want to perk up a sandwich, or want to add an extra element to a lettuce you've bought, simply clip

leaves off your salad pot, working your way round it. When the pot starts to look a bit ragged either cut all the lettuces at the base and use them in a final glorious salad, or use as a cooked vegetable (see Recipes, page 138). Then simply refresh the soil by taking out the bigger roots and adding fresh compost, sow more seeds and the cycle can begin again. Other mixes worth trying are Oriental Saladini and mesclun, or stir fry mixes. All will look fabulous, and give lots of gourmet delight. Spicy and braising mixes are sold for stir frying, but also make delicious winter salads.

Containers

Small gardens often have a relatively large area of hard surface, and crowded beds. Growing edibles in containers is a great way to introduce new plants into a garden like this. Containers have many advantages, including the way they can bring different heights to a garden, raising plants in the air and presenting a surface for trailing plants to fall down over. It can be very attractive contrasting the colours of pots and plants – a courgette with golden fruit such as Goldrush grown in a blue ceramic container looks marvellous, as the blue

Above **Although there's no grass in this Urban Eden, it is still a great place in which to play.**
Right **One of the joys of growing tomatoes is that many varieties bear fruits that do not all ripen at once, so you can pick fresh produce over a long period.**

background perfectly sets off the yellow flowers and fruit. Complementary colours are successful too, such as dusky sage in an old terracotta pot.

Courgettes highlight another reason containers really suit Urban Eden gardening: you can get the compost just right for the plant. Courgettes are incredibly greedy, and in a container the soil can be loaded with lots of well-rotted manure, more than most plants might feel comfortable with. At the end of the growing season, the compost from the pot is just about right for most other plants, so can go straight out onto beds.

Large containers If you have a big container in a sunny position, fill it to overflowing with a selection such as courgettes, strawberries and nasturtiums for vegetables, fruit, flowers and salad all at once. To get juicy and sweet strawberries for the whole of summer, use a mix of early, mid and late such as Roneoye, Cambridge Favourite and Cambridge Late Pine. A red nasturtium such as Empress of India or Gleaming Mahogany would look striking in this planting.

Maintenance Intense planting does require a certain amount of maintenance, especially very regular watering, and regular feeding. Also, the margin for error in containers is not very high. When a plant is in a bed and it gets hot and the soil begins to dry, you've got quite a bit of time before the soil dries all the way down to the subsoil and the plant succumbs to drought. In a container, when weather gets hot and the soil dries out death can be close at hand. To reduce the risk use a plastic bottle as described on page 17.

Crops The versatility of containers means that you can mix and match crops much more easily than when growing in open ground. You can use them to grow plants which crop well and quickly, look great, and can then be replaced with a completely different display. After the courgette and nasturtiums, for example, have passed their best, they could be replaced with a mass planting of rhubarb or ruby chard which has startling red leaf stems and dark-green crinkled leaves. Sow the seeds in later summer and plant in the container when they are between 2 and 5cm (1 and 2in) tall. Start fertilising after about a month's growth. They will survive a light frost, but may die back to crowns in very cold weather. They should sprout back again in spring.

Potatoes You can grow a crop of potatoes very successfully in a large container half filled with compost or soil in a shady garden. Plant a sprouting potato or two in spring – James uses

green sprouting ones from the kitchen but this practice does not work for everyone; you may be more successful with seed potatoes from a catalogue or garden centre. Peat-based compost can be convenient as it is light and you don't damage the tubers if you crop continuously, but potatoes are greedy and plants will need to be dosed regularly with a blood, fish and bone meal dressing which is high in phosphates and encourages the formation of healthy roots. Another alternative is to plant in rich well-manured soil. A potato plant will appear within a few weeks of planting and will grow well

Below Fruit trees can be grown successfully in containers. Choose something that either responds well to root restriction like a fig or, if it is a grafted plant like an apple, cherry or plum, choose a rootstock that is very dwarfing which naturally keeps the plant smaller.

as long as you keep watering. If possible, keep adding earth to the surface of the pot, mounding it up around the base of the potato stem. For a bigger crop, you can plant more potatoes in this mounded earth, and keep earthing upwards and planting more.

For much of its life, a potato plant is a mass of green, sappy shoots and looks good at the rear of an arrangement of pots, creating a green backdrop for other more striking plants. By midsummer, the tubers will start to form, and you can just feel around the base of the stems with your hands for the potatoes as they grow; pull a few at a time from the earth and let the plants keep growing. Or one day, to mark a celebration, tip the whole pot out and search through the earth for the crop, enough to entertain several people to a meal of absolutely fresh potatoes in the heart of town. Served with fresh garlic, parsley and butter, what could be better?

Fruit Large containers don't have to be used just for annuals: you can use them for permanent plantings, and many fruit trees are quite happy growing in containers. Apples and plums in particular thrive as long as they are on the right dwarfing

root stock (see page 46). Figs actually crop best when grown in containers, and quinces are quite content.

A standard gooseberry will be quite at home in a shady large container. Raising the plant above ground shows off its fruit which are otherwise hidden by the leaves and reduces the risk of mildew. Underplanted with oak leaf lettuce, blue violas and curly parsley, you would have a dramatic and productive selection.

Small containers Small containers are ideal for a wide range of plants.

Tomatoes These are extremely good in pots on tall windowsills, in sunny gardens, and on sheltered roofs and balconies, and you can choose from a huge range of different-coloured varieties with different habits, from small and bushy to tall and elegant. Simply keep them well fed and watered, stake if necessary and stop their growth to encourage heavy crops when they are flowering profusely by nipping out the top shoots. Don't be tempted to put tomatoes into large pots, the more you restrict their roots, the better they fruit.

Below Once you start growing a range of edible plants you soon realise that they can be every bit as beautiful as more conventional ornamental plants. You may decide to choose what edibles to grow according to their shapes, colours and seasons as well as for their flavours.

Peppers Peppers also grow very successfully in pots in sunny situations. They are lovely plants, easy to grow from seed into a fine branching form with pretty leaves, white and yellow flowers and plentiful fruit. It can be amusing to play visual jokes with striking coloured and shaped plants: you could for example grow a hot chilli pepper in a red fire bucket in the hottest part of the garden.

Shallots Shallots grow well in a small container in a sunny spot. Plant a sprouting shallot in the spring, and up will come a circle of dazzling bright green spears. And when you suddenly decide to make a dish which cries out for a shallot, it is a real thrill to pop out into the garden, and simply grab one from the pot!

Garlic In winter, containers could play host to garlic. Plant two or three cloves in medium-sized pots larger than 15cm (6in) in fairly rich compost, water them in and leave them to overwinter, making sure the soil doesn't dry out. In spring green shoots will emerge, turning into what look like mini leeks. You can leave them in pots or transfer them into the garden as garlic likes food and space. Container-grown garlic is every bit as good as ground-grown; but the bulbs may be smaller. By midsummer the garlic shoots will start to wither, a sign that the plants have reached the end of their natural growth cycle. At this point, empty the pot and retrieve a small bulb of garlic at the end of each shoot. Enjoy it while it is fresh, it is much sharper than the semi-dried garlic we are used to.

Mint In a shady spot, small containers are ideal for mints, and there are lots of interesting and useful varieties. Mints are ideal for pots: it means they can't spread and bully other plants out of the beds, and you can place containers so that you brush past them regularly and fill the air with scent.

Another approach is to add to existing ornamental plants in containers. If you have a red rose in a pot, try underplanting with coriander. Instead of stopping the coriander flowering, let the flowers bloom. Their delicate white tracery sets off the darker red roses marvellously.

Mobility With a good variety of Urban Eden containers going, you can have great fun in the garden, creating a constantly changing and attractive scene. The best-looking plants can be moved so you can enjoy them in your main view. They can be placed at different levels, on the ground, steps or tables for different effects. The ones that need sun to ripen fruit can be moved into the warmest position, and plants that prefer a bit of shade can be nestled under the shadow of sun-lovers. This mobility has other virtues: Adam had some beans planted in beds and some in pots and when there was a ferociously destructive wind one early summer evening he was able to move the beans in the pots into a sheltered position. The ones in the beds were shredded but the ones in the pots survived to produce a superb crop.

Fruit in containers

The exciting thing about growing fruit in containers is that it expands the possibilities of what you can grow in your garden. For instance, in climates where the winter would kill a lemon or orange, it is possible to grow them successfully in a container and bring them indoors, to a cool light room, in winter. Peaches and nectarines, which suffer from leaf curl if rained on while their buds are swelling, can be brought under cover during the critical weeks if grown in a container. In areas without acid soils, blueberries make a fine specimen in a container of ericaceous (acidic) compost.

Another great advantage of growing fruit in containers is that they can be moved about the garden (see page 80). When they are flowering and fruiting they can be put in the main view. It is tremendously exciting to watch your own peaches reddening in the sun, day by day, waiting for the moment when you are going to pluck them from the tree.

Apples, cherries, pears and the various plums are grafted onto rootstocks which determine the size of the mature tree

Right This pear tree makes an attractive feature at any time of year, whether it's bare, in flower, in leaf or in fruit. Unfortunately this year's crop will not feed the family. The rosemary, however, that shares the pot and encourages beneficial insects to the tree, is doing brilliantly, and there's always next year to look forward to.

Above **Fill containers on a balcony with scented plants and make a perfect corner to sit and enjoy the sun.**
Right **On this sheltered balcony citrus and banana enjoy being out in summer, but in all but the warmest climates they need to be moved indoors for winter protection.**

and control the rate of growth. If you want to grow tree fruit in containers, look for rootstock such as the very dwarfing Pixie for apples, plums, cherries, peaches and nectarines, dwarfing M27 for apples and Tabel for cherries. A good dwarfing rootstock will probably be available for pears soon as new stocks are being trialled all the time, but at present it is better to grow pears trained either as cordons or espaliers, if you have limited space. When choosing fruit to grow in a pot, look for varieties that are self-fertile and disease-resistant. Red Falstaff is a reliable apple, and Celeste and Stella are good cherries. There are also all sorts of new varieties that have been specially developed for container growing including space-saving pole-shaped trees with all the fruits clustering around a central stem.

Balconies

Most balconies are fairly small, and the temptation is to fill the limited space with numerous small pots. However, the conditions here can be quite extreme as the wind lashes around buildings, knocking things over, and drying everything out quickly. So it is much better to use larger pots, as long as the structure can stand it, as they tend to anchor plants better and will hold the water for much longer. Generous pots with larger specimens can also provide a bit of shade and shelter from the wind, creating an ideal place in which to cluster a few smaller pots.

Wind The best way of coping with the wind is to create a wind-break by putting a large, wind-tolerant plant in the direct path of the prevailing wind to disrupt the flow. An evergreen pink- or red-flowered *Escallonia* would be a good decorative choice which can be regularly clipped to keep it in check. The scented white-flowered *Escallonia iveyii* is unfortunately less hardy and would suffer. Many cotoneasters also tolerate wind and create some shelter, and can be attractive with their small evergreen leaves, white flowers and red berries. They can also be trained flat to take up minimal space.

Figs Low-growing plants such as salad pots (see page 38) are ideal for balconies. But you don't have to restrict yourself to small plants. How about growing a fig on a balcony in a sheltered corner? Figs have delicious fruit, dramatically lobed leaves which are slightly aromatic in the sun, and a grey bloom on the bark. Figs perform best when their roots are restricted in a pot about 45cm (18in) deep and fruit quite freely in milder climates; the hardiest outdoor varieties for cooler areas are Brown Turkey and White Marseilles. Since figs are quite

substantial plants and weight can be a problem on a balcony, use a lightweight soil-less compost in a plastic pot. Feed and water well throughout the spring and summer as figs are hungry feeders.

To encourage maximum fruit production, you can prune the fig stems back to four or five leaves in summer. And in late summer remove any little hard fig fruits left on the plant as these will survive over the winter, swell a bit in spring, but won't develop into edible fruit. Removing them saves the

Left Balconies suffer from wind, and plants must be securely tied to avoid damage. Branches bearing a heavy apple crop should be supported in even a sheltered position in case the weight of the fruit causes the branch to split.

Below left Figs are relatively hardy but adore the sun. Some people recommend stripping some of the leaves from around the fruit to give maximum exposure to sun.

plant energy, which will increase the edible crop. Once figs appear in spring, they swell surprisingly quickly. If necessary, removing a few leaves from around each fig will help the fruit to ripen, and will not harm the plant as long as it is done in moderation. In a good summer, with a fig that is a few years old, you can expect dozens of figs towards the end of the summer. Of course, in cool climates, or when the summer fails to arrive, or in a shaded position, the figs may not ripen at all, but they are such fine-looking plants, so evocative of hot countries, that they are still worth growing in a pot. Then, should you move, or get access to somewhere sunnier, you'll have a mature fig tree, in a pot, ready to start giving you fruit in summer.

Hanging baskets Hanging baskets, or on windier balconies, wall planters, offer a lot of opportunities, as they make use of the vertical dimension.

Tomatoes In a sunny position you can get superb crops of tomatoes from Tumbler tomatoes, a variety bred specially for baskets. It is a prolific cropper, with excellent flavour and bunches of glossy red globes spill over the edge of the basket for weeks and weeks in summer. The hanging basket can be enhanced by teaming the tomato up with a plant that won't compete too much for water and nutrients such as trailing *Lobelia* 'Regatta Blue Splash'. Feed the basket once a week when the first fruits set, and keep evenly moist, especially when the fruits are ripening. Turn it now and again so that each part of the basket gets its fair share of sun and air – a content Tumbler plant can produce an astonishing 4 kilos (9 lb) of fruit, so it is worth a little extra trouble.

Herbs Herbs do well too in a hanging basket. They love the sun and have excellent survival skills if you forget to water them now and again. While they are not exactly a riot of colour, they are quietly pleasing. Put some thymes round the edge of a basket – they will like the relatively drier conditions. The flowers are a bonus, and bees love them. For the centre of the basket take your pick from any of the lusher herbs such as chives and parsley, or even basil. Alternatively, put in young plants of rosemary and sage which appreciate the excellent drainage of hanging baskets. They can be transferred to the garden or larger pots when they outgrow their welcome. Keep all baskets well watered in hot weather, and pick regularly to keep everything in check. Do not use mint as it will attempt to annex the whole basket.

Strawberries In dappled shade (not deepest gloom) a hanging basket of alpine strawberries *Fragaria vesca semperflorens* will provide a lot of visual pleasure and fruit. Alpine strawberries are well suited to growing above ground where fewer pests can get at their fruit. They flower profusely all summer and produce a good quantity of fruits which are much smaller and less sweet than the commercial varieties, but much more tangy. Simply fill a moss-lined basket with a good strong

PRUNING AND TRAINING FRUIT TREES

Why prune? There are lots of different ways of training fruit trees including espaliers, fans, cordons and step-overs. All need to be pruned differently. However, the necessity to prune and train is much less than it was. With old varieties, fruit trees had to be pruned in the first few years to discourage fruiting which diverted energy from vegetative growth. When the framework was established, fruit trees had to be pruned to maximise fruit production and to limit growth. As the trees aged, pruning reduced the opportunities for diseases and pests and the incidence of biennial cropping.

New varieties With the introduction of new dwarfing root stocks and varieties which are more resistant to disease and biennial cropping, fruit trees can be allowed to fruit earlier, will keep to a modest size, and will remain relatively healthy. However, regular pruning will help to create a more productive and attractive tree. A couple of techniques are worth trying in a small garden.

Method The main aim of pruning and training fruit trees in borders is to allow as much light and air in as possible. Cut branches that point inwards to create a goblet shape. Try 'festooning', a system whereby branches are pulled down below the horizontal to encourage fruit production. This should be done while the wood is young and bends easily. Pull the branches down with wires, anchoring them by tying the wire round a thick cloth wrapped round the trunk.

If you like a more formal look, or have little space, try an upright cordon. This is a central trunk off which come short spurs which fruit heavily. This is mainly appropriate for apples and pears, but not for those that bear on the tips of branches. In early July, prune all the current season's growth back to two or three buds. Prune the regrowth again in winter. Done regularly, so that the tree is densely covered in spurs, it looks marvellous.

compost (a mix of soil-based and soil-less suits them) and sow the seed on the surface. The young plants grow quickly.

Roof gardens

The conditions on a roof are more extreme than anywhere else: windier, sunnier, drier in hot weather, and wetter when it rains. Without help, few plants will thrive in this cocktail of extremes. But with some preparation, a roof garden can be surprisingly productive.

What is needed is a convenient way of watering in the heat, some protection from the wind, and good drainage so that plants are not waterlogged in the cold. On a roof this might mean installing a watering system – or at the very least a tap; putting saucers under the pots in summer so that they retain water; some sort of wind-break, which might be several large plants round the perimeter, or a hurdle fence; and pot feet under containers in winter so they drain well when it rains. If you do all this, a roof garden can be a fantastic place to grow perennial Mediterranean herbs, vines, and annual crops that like lots of sun (shallots, tomatoes, basil, pepper).

However, the kitchen is often quite a way from the roof garden, so it makes less sense to grow vegetables, salads or herbs there unless you are extremely well organised or very fit. It is incredibly irritating to be cooking and realise a) the recipe demands a sprig of fresh tarragon, b) the tarragon is doing brilliantly on the roof, and c) that you are either going to have to climb all the way to the top of the house to get it, or leave it out of the dish! In this situation, it is best to grow things on the roof that can be enjoyed eaten straight off the plant.

Edibles in borders

Climbers Many edible plants look so ornamental that they need no justification for use in a border. Runner beans grown on a wigwam of bamboo canes are normally the preserve of a vegetable garden. But they look superb in an otherwise ornamental border. They can grow as high as the canes they are trained on, and always seem to want to go higher.

Right Although brassicas are rarely worth growing in a very small urban garden, coloured cabbages and kales look marvellous in an edible border, here combined with alliums, corn and other leafy greens as well as flowers.

Set against the red, translucent foliage of a *Cotinus* 'Royal Purple', the soft, elegant green leaves of the bean and the bright red flowers are a perfect match. The beans are best grown in the ground because they are greedy, but can be grown in a large container which can simply be moved into the border when they are well-established if you are prepared to water and feed them frequently. Half burying the container in the soil is a good way of reducing the risk of it drying out should you be unable to water it.

Climbing summer squash plants grown on a wigwam make a fantastic addition to any border. These are best established in a pot, and once climbing strongly and covered in fruit move them into the border. Their bright flowers and extraordinary fruit give a visual lift wherever they are placed.

Eye-catching plants The amazing dark-green crinkly leaves of a healthy curly kale *Brassica oleracea* seem to absorb the light; they are superb with mound-forming ornamentals like the grey-foliaged *Senecio* 'Sunshine'. A clump of the incredibly vivid-coloured ruby chard is a good addition to most borders. Or you can now even buy seeds for an eyecatching rainbow-coloured variety with stems in yellow, orange, purple, and pink and white stripes.

Sage *Salvia officinalis* is another eye-catching option, especially its purple-leafed form *S. purpurascens*, and the

variegated *S. icterina*. Sage plants often seem to do vigorously for about three years, and then get old and fade away. It is best simply to replace them. Luckily, sage layers easily: that is, forms roots where branches touch the soil. So after a couple of years' growth, pin a long shoot of sage down to the ground without cutting it from the main plant. After six months, that shoot should have rooted, and you can cut it from the parent shrub and plant it somewhere else. When the parent gets tired, you have a young plant to take over, but it is best not to plant the new sage in exactly the same place. The upright forms of rosemary are also lovely shrubs. The branches of Miss Jessopp's Upright reach upwards in a very appealing way and given fertile, well-drained soil and a sunny position can be very vigorous, providing masses of rosemary for the kitchen.

A small practical point, born of experience. If you put a herb plant in a border by a prickly plant, you will get scratched when you dash out at night for a leaf or two to add to a dish.

Bold plantings If a border needs something architectural to spruce it up, a bay tree *Laurus nobilis* is a good choice. They grow well as long as they are sheltered from too much wind, and so the town garden is ideal for them. They tolerate clipping, so once they are established, they invite a spot of topiary and they look fine all year round. Fennel *Foeniculum vulgare* is another striking addition to a sunny, moist border. Its delicate frond-like leaves shoot up very enthusiastically in spring, and it has pretty yellow flowerheads in summer. The bronze variety is a good foil against pale greens in a border.

If you have a bright sunny border, where you want to make a bold statement, you could try a stand of sweetcorn *Zea mays*. It doesn't thrive in cool wet summers, and needs rich soil, but in a hot summer you will benefit from tall attractive plants with delicious corns as a bonus. You should plant at least six together so that they can pollinate each other, and you will have the best chance of getting several cobs ripening at once.

If you have the space, an artichoke *Cynara scolymus* provides ideal spot interest, providing height and stature in a border.

This stunning perennial can grow to 1.5m (5ft) or more in good rich soil and a bright, sunny position. It has amazing silvery green deeply cut leaves, exotic flowers which taste wonderful in bud, and are fringed with bright purple if not cropped. Asparagus *Asparagus officinalis* is another splendid plant with fronds that, allowed to develop fully, form an elegant backdrop for summer annuals. Asparagus needs very deep rich soil, and takes two years to crop from crowns, and unless your garden is fairly large you will not glean many meals of it, but if you have a spare square metre (3ft square) of bed it is tremendously exciting to crop a handful of the delicious spears in spring as they push through the ground ahead of any other produce.

Herbaceous borders In an herbaceous border, borage *Borago officinalis,* is a very attractive plant. Its leaf is slightly hairy, but when picked young is a good addition to a mixed summer salad, and gives a slight taste of cucumber to a summer cordial. The bright, star-shaped blue flowers combine beautifully with the blue-tinged hostas, especially one of the more compact forms like Blue Wedgewood which grows to only 25cm (10in). To complete the picture, add a further contrast with an underplanting of ground-hugging *Ajuga reptans* 'Multicolour', giving a wash of cream-splashed purple leaves, and a spring bonus of dark-blue flower-spikes. A low-growing *Tradescantia* would be fun too, especially one of the purple-leafed forms like *Tradescantia pallida* 'Purpurea'. Although borage is an annual, it self-seeds and so will come back year after year.

Fruit trees

Fruit trees, such as an apples, cherries or pears are a very valuable addition to any garden. The pear, for instance, is a magnificent tree when mature, has a lovely shape, is breathtaking in flower, with bark that looks like ancient bark mosaic. And it bears delicious fruit. Peaches and apricots often grow well in warm sheltered town gardens.

You could also consider more unusual fruit trees. A

mulberry *Morus nigra* would not be suitable for the smallest gardens because, although it is very slow growing, it would eventually outshade the rest of the garden. But if you have a suitable site, this beautiful tree is well worth considering. It is disease-free, does not need pruning and looks mature very quickly; but mulberries need a lot of care, especially careful watering, and hate any disturbance near their roots; they do not fruit until they are at least 15 years old. Medlars are delightful trees, with dense rounded canopies and

Below **Every Urban Eden should make room for at least one fruit tree (and more if possible). A blossoming tree has a modest beauty that puts some of the more gaudy ornamentals to shame and a tree full of fruit is a glorious sight.**

Above **Man-made colour
can complement the
colours of nature. Here the
green wall is soothing and
blends the boundary into
the bed in front of it and
the over-hanging bushes.**
Above right **The white walls
lighten this corner and
help to make the pots
stand out from the
background.**

extraordinary fruit, and they are easy to grow. Quince is also
very attractive, with lovely flowers, and highly scented fruit
which makes a delicious preserve (see Recipes, page 141).
Quince and medlar both look superb in autumn.

Getting a good crop from a fruit tree does require slightly
more commitment from the gardener than growing a purely
ornamental one. The blooms of the early flowering ones,
including most plums, may require protection from frost, and
once the fruit has set, the tree may have to be protected against
birds. Although many are naturally quite susceptible to pests
and disease, because the Urban Eden gardener is not growing
for show, most of these can be tolerated.

Growing hints Fruit trees can be grown in a number of ways depending on the space you have available: in containers; free-standing; trained into shapes or grown against a wall. Well-trained fruit trees can look very stylish. In a border in a small garden you should probably choose a dwarf rootstock which means that after ten years the tree will be less than 3m (10ft) high. Trees grown on semi-dwarf rootstock will grow to about half a metre (18in) more.

All fruit trees apart from Morello cherries benefit from sun. In temperate climates, peaches and nectarines are best grown on the sunniest wall in the garden. Pears and damsons will tolerate a shady position, but their fruit will not be very sweet. Many apples, cherries, pears and plums require a compatible tree nearby that will provide pollen in order for the flowers to set into fruit. For the most part, the urban environment has so many trees in it of so many sorts that this should not be a major concern. However if there are few gardens around you, or few trees in those gardens, look for a self-fertile variety, or buy a pair of fruit trees that will fertilise each other.

Walls

In the small Urban Eden, there is often proportionally a good deal of wall for the bed space. Walls are actually a great boon: after all, people used to go to great expense to build walled gardens because a sunny wall is sunnier and warmer and more sheltered than other places in the garden. Set against that is the fact that a shady wall is shadier, and that plants grown against walls can suffer from drought caused by rain shadow.

To show to best advantage In order to make the best use of a wall, train wires along it parallel to the ground at intervals of 30cm (12in) or so. You can tie plants into this as they grow. Apples and pears grow well on walls trained as espaliers with branches stretched out horizontally either side of the trunk and the side shoots pruned back to make fruiting spurs. They look lovely underplanted with garlic chives, or other low-growing herbs that like sun and don't require too much water.

An exciting combination is climbing Little Gem squash and blue morning glories underplanted with borage which will give a glorious and productive display of yellows and blues throughout the summer.

You could train many of the beans on a sunny wall; they look fantastic with the purple morning glories, especially against a white wall. Tomatoes can also be surprisingly attractive trained against a wall, their star-shaped rather insignificant lemon-yellow flowers greatly enhanced by combining them with something with contrasting star-shaped flowers like passion flower *Passiflora* 'Lavender Lady'.

Sun and shade South-facing walls are perfect for peaches, apricots, plums and greengages trained in a fan shape so that they grow flat against the wall. This means they take up very little bed space. As the tree grows, tie in new growth, pruning off only dead and diseased branches, branches that grow outwards over the bed, or that cross other branches. Soft fruit is also ideal for a warm wall. Fan-train a red currant against a wall and put bronze fennel in front of it. Red currants fruit on spurs, and the currants hang from the plant like long, dangling earrings. After it has fruited, the bronze fennel will look magnificent, its yellow flowers contrasting with its reddish feathery foliage. Add Harlequin marigolds (which have red and yellow flowers in summer) and underplant with orange tiger lilies *Lilium tigrinum* which will erupt with orange flowers.

A Morello cherry will thrive on a shady wall, producing cooking cherries which are sour, but delicious in pies, tarts, puddings and jam.

To encourage tree growth When planting a fruit tree, particularly near a wall, sink a large pot with holes in the bottom into the earth beside the roots. To keep the tree adequately hydrated, fill this empty pot to the brim with water. This encourages the new roots to go downwards. After a year or two you can remove this pot as by then the tree should be well established and able to fend for itself.

Ground cover

Ground cover in larger gardens is used because there is so much bed space to fill and plants are needed that will keep low, look after themselves and grow sufficiently densely to keep the weeds down. The usual ground cover plants are ajugas, euphorbias, geraniums, pachysandra, pulmonarias and vincas. These are all quite vigorous, and groups of them can cover a large area. Visually they are used to link bigger shrubs and trees.

Relatively few Urban Eden gardeners have large spaces like this which require filling. What most do have, however, are empty pockets in borders, and a few difficult-to-garden areas for instance, the dry shade under a tree near a wall. So most Urban Eden gardeners are looking for space fillers rather than the traditional ground cover.

Sun-loving plants   In relatively sunny spots, trailing rosemary *Rosmarinus officinalis* 'Severn Sea' is a great choice. With its dense evergreen foliage of needle-like leaves and vivid blue flowers, it is both a useful culinary plant and very ornamental ground cover. Common thyme is good ground cover if the soil is well drained and winters are not too cold and damp, and there are lots of ornamental thymes such as *Thymus vulgaris* 'Silver Posie' with its pale pink/lilac flowers in summer, and leaves variegated with grey.

Chamomile *Chamaemelum nobile* is an excellent ground-cover plant for full or dappled sun as it stays very low, is evergreen and very dense. The leaves have an almost luminous intensity of green, and are sweetly aromatic. If you want to make your own chamomile tea, make sure you choose one of the flowering varieties.

Rocket *Eruca vesicaria* planted in clumps is a marvellous quick way to fill spare space, and is delicious. It needs regular cropping if it is not to flower and run to seed. Basil can even go in spare patches of sunny soil. Where slugs and snails are a problem, the plants will get eaten, but the leaves that remain are a welcome addition to a summer salad. Nasturtiums are marvellous ground cover in sunny spots. They've got it all: the flowers are brilliantly coloured and the flowers, seeds and leaves are a peppery addition to a salad.

Shade-loving plants   For ground cover in the shade, buckler leafed sorrel *Rumex scutatus* is low-growing with pale-green leaves shaped like medieval shields. It forms pretty clumps, and trails attractively. The larger sorrel *Rumex acetosa* also covers shady ground well with its pleasing spear-shaped bright-green leaves.

Wild garlic *Allium ursinum* is a superb way of filling a shady area and its leaves are a fine addition to a salad. But don't plant it in a very damp garden or it can become invasive as it self-seeds. In a damp Urban Eden, soup celery *Apium graveolens* 'French Dinant' is a valuable plant. It grows well in semi-shade, providing leaves and stems that taste strongly of celery, a perfect substitute in all those recipes that require 'one stick of celery'. It is very hardy and self-seeds quite freely without becoming invasive.

Mint can be used as a shady spacefiller but be careful which variety you plant or your garden will be taken over. Pineapple mint *Mentha suaveolens variegata* has very attractive white and green leaves, and is not as rampant as many of its relatives. Comfrey *Symphytum officinale* will survive in the very difficult position under a tree and by a wall. Comfrey is attractive, having clusters of flowers which vary between white, purple and pink, and is very useful in any garden for fertiliser. If you steep cut comfrey leaves in water for four weeks, you will have a powerful organic fertiliser full of potash. Added to the compost heap, they speed the process of composting. Although the leaves are edible, they are not to everyone's taste – even a couple of helpings in any one year is more than enough for most people!

One further point is worth making. You do not have to fill every space in your borders, but leave some empty. You may want to grow some annuals, or need somewhere to put plants in pots as they travel around the garden (see page 80).

Below **Massed chives
make a splendid show
as ground cover in an
area that rarely gets
walked on, and gets
little attention apart
from irregular watering.**

4 The urban landscape · Existing features · Eyesores · Boundaries · Sun & shade · Bed layout
Large versus small plants · Hard landscaping & grass · Vertical elements · Scent · Garden as gallery · Surprises
All-year-round views · Topiary · Case histories

design

The design of a small garden in a town or city is not the same – or at least it should not be – as the design of a garden in the countryside. There are different pressures and different features to be taken into account.In the city, for instance, with hardly any green space in which to relax and recharge your batteries, a garden is more than just a place to grow plants. It is a retreat, a place in which to commune with nature, a place to recover from the frustrations of city life.

Also, most urban gardens are comparatively small. The process and principles that underpin the design of a small garden are not the same as those that apply to a big garden. With a big garden, a large part of the design challenge is usually how to fill up the space and minimise maintenance. With a small garden, particularly one in the urban environment, the challenge is often how to get more into the garden, while still minimising maintenance.

Incorporating vegetables, fruit, herbs and salads into the mix enriches it further, but necessitates a whole new set of thoughts when considering design.

What follows are some principles to help you design and change your garden so that, given your taste and your resources (time, money, energy and horticultural knowledge), your garden will be both visually delightful, and productive and will work excellently in a modern, urbanised environment.

The urban landscape

The urban landscape is emphatically not just traffic and skyscrapers. It is much more interesting than that. Most urban gardens are set amongst other urban gardens, a network of spaces in which many keen and knowledgeable gardeners have, over the years, planted small trees and shrubs and nurtured them into breathtaking specimens. Around this patchwork of gardens are often, in the distant background, the mature trees that line streets and fill parks. It is usually a dense, varied landscaping, featuring a fascinating and often exotic mix of greenery and buildings. It is typical of the city: crowded, vibrant, with beauty juxtaposed with eyesores.

This landscape is one of the most powerful visual features of many urban gardens. The design of an Urban Eden seeks to make the most of that, and to enable the urban gardener to use to the full whatever garden is available.

Styling At its best, the urban environment is a vibrant mix of different cultures, traditions and styles. The Urban Eden garden can reflect that diversity. Instead of just having a single, rigid style – for instance, the classic all-white garden, or a potager – the Urban Eden garden can look wonderful by borrowing, mixing and matching from all sorts of styles and traditions. A tropical plant, juxtaposed with a shrub that has been topiarised, under a wild-looking tree, with herbs in pots set around the base can look perfectly harmonious. Just as modern cooking is fusion cooking, this is a form of fusion gardening.

The Urban Eden attitude is that design is a process, part of almost everything done in the garden, not something done once and then never again. Plants grow into and around each other. Things happen by chance. By constantly looking and adjusting, and allowing plants to do their own thing, you can get some novel and delightful combinations. For instance, a *Kerria japonica* was growing near a bay tree *Laurus nobilis*. The *Kerria* is a spring-flowering shrub, which has yellow pompom flowers on shoots normally 2m (6ft) high. It spreads by

suckers, and had started to grow into and through the bay. It is unlikely that anyone would have planned this, but it was allowed to continue. What happened was that the bay tree branches supported the *Kerria* sprays. After a couple of years, the *Kerria* had worked its way up to the top of the bay tree – a full 6m (20ft) or more above ground. The result is that in spring, yellow *Kerria* pompoms erupt out of the bay here and there right up to the top. It's a lovely sight, both surprising and delightful. It isn't harming the bay, and the *Kerria* too seems very happy.

Existing features

When designing an Urban Eden it is important to look beyond your immediate boundaries for dominant features in neighbouring gardens. Unless your need for privacy overwhelms every other concern, incorporating them into the design of your garden is a powerful technique for expanding your vista.

For instance, if a large ash tree *Fraxinus excelsior* of perhaps 10m (33ft) is visible from your garden you can make a link to it by planting a smaller tree in your garden so that the two are

Above left Make a small basement garden feel bigger with clean shapes and uncluttered planting. *Above centre* In a small, long garden surrounded by mature trees, the challenge is how to make them increase the feeling of space in your garden. *Above* With a view like this, just soften a few edges but don't obscure it.

seen together when looking from the main viewpoint in your garden. If you chose a *Sorbus villmorinii*, its fern-like foliage, bronze autumn colours and pink berries, which fade to almost pure white, would stand out against the pale green of the ash, which would be the perfect backdrop for this small showy star. Although the *Sorbus* does take up quite a lot of room, its effect in this position – paradoxically – would be to expand the view greatly.

Or imagine that you could see a large *Magnolia soulangiana* from your garden. It looks wonderful in spring while in bud and flower, but for the rest of the year is fairly plain. One option would be to create a stunning spring display by planting a smaller, white-flowering shrub in your garden. The lilac buds and flushed white flowers of *Rhododendron* 'Loder's White' would link superbly with the white and purple of the magnolia. However, this planting would look relatively humdrum for much of the year; a more Urban Eden design would be to allow the magnolia to star while it flowers, and then be the backdrop when in full leaf to something in your garden with a similar shape. The Japanese maple *Acer palmatum* 'Osakazuki' would work very well with its summer and autumn interest. It has delicate lobed leaves in the summer, and stunning orange and reds in autumn.

If a tall, narrow, columnar tree such as a Lombardy poplar *Populus nigra* 'Italica' was in your line of vision you could make the most if it by planting a shrub or tree in your garden with a contrasting shape. A weeping ornamental pear *Pyrus salicifolia* 'Pendula' with its soft, silky, downy grey foliage would be superb. It forms itself into a mound, and would set off the exclamation mark of the poplar beautifully.

Large trees A surprising number of small gardens contain relatively large trees. They have often been planted years ago, and just left to get on with it. But if a tree is neglected for too

Above **Even though this garden is small, the simple design enables produce to be grown and consumed in the same space – a particularly delightful experience.**
Above right **Vegetables can be astonishingly ornamental.**

long, it can become overgrown, diseased, lop-sided and quite unattractive. So for many people – especially men – the answer is simple: 'Bring me a chain saw and stand well back.' But increasingly people are getting more and more reluctant to take down a tree. This seems reasonable: the world needs more trees. In design terms it makes sense too: a large feature like a tree, which has taken a long time to form, could be the focal point of the whole garden. With a tree that has got out of hand the question should be: can you make something positive out of it?

Solutions For instance, will good treatment remedy the situation? With a tree up to 3m (10ft), you can probably do it yourself. Cut out all diseased branches (those where the bark is cracked, and the leaves are sparse and wilting) and any that cross other branches. The aim is to create an open structure, with branches radiating out from the trunk, to introduce light and air into the heart of the tree. Give it a good feed of an all-round plant food every three or four years. With a neglected tree of over 4m (13ft) consult a professional tree surgeon before taking action. They can advise on the best way to proceed.

If the tree is healthy, but is not providing enough interest, use it to support a flowering or fruiting climber. A spring-flowering cherry tree may take up a lot of room, but only gives interest in one season so you could grow a flowering climber like *Clematis orientalis* up it. This would create two seasons of interest: spring when the tree flowers, and late summer when the nodding yellow flowers of the clematis will cascade from the tree followed by ethereal silvery seed-heads. Never introduce something into the tree that will overwhelm it. Russian vine *Polygonum baldschuanicum*, for instance, would

Left Ordinary plastic mesh will be transformed into a stunning feature when covered with sweet peas and runner beans.

Below Even when not in flower, this wisteria helps to screen the building behind, and softens the verticals of the railings.

Right The need to conceal a drainpipe against a wall has inspired an Urban Eden planting with hops and thyme.

Eyesores

Most urban views also feature an eyesore or two. It might just be the neighbour's garage, or a washing line, but once noticed it's like a dripping tap, a constant focus of irritation. It's tempting to plant a quick-growing screen in front of it, at its most extreme something like *Cupressus leylandii*. Unfortunately, precisely because these plants are quick-growing, they become very tall and consequently take a great deal of light, water and nutrition from your garden. They, in their turn, become dominant, and an eyesore for you and for others.

Screening It is usually better partially to screen anything unsightly. You could plant one of the quinces like *Cydonia* 'Vranja'. Although it is slow-growing, it will attract the eye from early on in its life with its large apple-like blossom, its large yellow fruit and downy, delicate soft-green leaves. In winter, when the quince is bare, distract the eye completely by planting something magnificent in another part of the garden. *Mahonia* 'Charity' with masses of spiky yellow flowers erupting in a fountain from its tower of holly-like leaves would be a perfect choice.

If you haven't space for a shrub or tree, a trellis placed in front of the eyesore with a climber growing up it makes a very good screen. Go for something wonderful rather than something that grows too quickly. For instance, the evergreen *Trachelospermum jasminoides* has strongly scented flowers for three months in summer and will relish a hot position.

Many honeysuckles are also excellent screens, although they do best where the soil is fertile. *Lonicera halliana* has powerfully scented yellow flowers all summer, and keeps its leaves except in a cold winter. If the winter view is not that important a spot that is hot in summer is ideal for a grape vine, or in a shady situation *Clematis montana* 'Tetrarose' has foaming masses of soft pink flowers in spring, and new growth tinged with red.

grow so vigorously that the cherry would be at risk after a couple of years.

Sometimes a big tree really does have to be removed. Before doing so, tell your neighbours. That tree forms part of their vista, and if one day it simply disappears, they can be angry and shocked. Also, large trees in some circumstances are protected by law. So consult your local authority to make sure you are entitled to cut it down.

Boundaries

The boundaries of an Urban Eden should be much more than just the legal and physical separation between you and your neighbours. There's so much more that can be done with them other than just leaving them as a simple wall or fence, or covering them with a fast-growing evergreen climber.

Disguise Where the existing boundary is unsightly, it can be covered with a productive and interesting plant. Golden hop *Humulus lupulus* 'Aureus' is a vigorous climber with leaves that glow golden in the sunshine. It bears a few, lightly scented bunches of hops and dies back to the ground in winter. *Jasminium officinalis* has clusters of white flowers with a heady scent; *Akebia quinata* is a twining evergreen with purple dangling flowers in late winter. Both grow well through and up trellis or chain-link. Blackberry 'Oregon Thornless' can be grown as part of a boundary, but it does need tying in.

Avoid anything that is too vigorous that could cause your neighbours a problem. No-one will thank you for putting a Russian vine on a boundary, as it can easily get out of control and rampage into others' plants. Even something beautiful can become a nuisance if it is too vigorous for a small garden, or too near the neighbours. *Rosa* 'Kiftsgate' and *R*. 'Wedding Day' are lovely in flower, but grow at an astonishing rate, and up to a huge height. They can take over a neighbour's tree, and cause no end of problems.

Decoration Another way of improving an unattractive existing boundary of wood or concrete is to paint it with a colour. Coloured wood stains also help weatherproof a fence. Changing the colour of a boundary can make a dramatic difference to the feel of the whole garden. There are no hard-and-fast rules about colour, but some general points are worth noting. White reflects the light, lifting the garden visually; it is excellent in the sun, but can look a bit dingy in shade. Primary colours tend to be most appropriate where there is a lot of sun, where they can sing out in the bright light. Pastel shades and darker colours work best in shadier areas, where the more muted light suits their softer tones. Green can be a very good background, as it merges in with the dominant tones in the garden, and adds a serene feeling where it is more exposed. Green works particularly well in small gardens when there is a lot of hard surface and no grass.

Those of artistic bent can use a fence as a canvas for a trompe l'oeil, or make a mosaic with all sorts of different materials: shells, pebbles, even different-coloured woods, and fix it to a wall. These techniques give greater depth to a small garden, and work equally well in the shade or in the sun. But a poorly executed trompe l'oeil is a permanent embarrassment so don't attempt it if in doubt!

If the garden is very small, you can fool the eye with a carefully placed mirror on a wall to create the illusion of space. This works best away from the main view, where the edges of the mirrors are concealed by planting, and another plant or structure obscures some of the mirror.

Playing with heights More radical choices are to lower an oppressive wall or fence, and use shrubs to get privacy, or to break any uniformity by having one or several sides of the garden – or panels of fence – at different heights. The best shrubs are those that don't get too wide or are easily clipped. Fast-growing ones are a nuisance. A mixed planting can give prolonged interest: try including a rambling or climbing rose like 'New Dawn' with fragrant blush-pink flowers all summer and attractive foliage; *Viburnum bodnantense* 'Dawn', a tall-growing 2m (6ft 6in) woody shrub with intensely scented pink pompom flowers in midwinter and *Pyracantha* 'Mojave' a very hardy prickly evergreen with white flowers in spring and glorious red-orange berries in autumn.

If a wall or fence forms an unbroken horizontal line all round the garden, it is a good idea to interrupt the top of it. Breaking the line with a tall shrub or tree will reduce its impact, stopping your garden from feeling boxed in. *Prunus* 'Amanogawa' grows up to 6m (20ft) with a narrow, columnar

habit and semi-double creamy-pink flowers in spring. A bamboo like *Phyllostachys nigra* could be interesting, with its black stems and pale, evergreen foliage.

Using walls With a tall wall as one of your boundaries, you could plant one of the aerial rooting plants like a self-clinging ivy or the Virgina creeper *Parthenocissus quinquefolia*, or its slower relative *P. Henryana* which has a more interesting leaf. *Hydrangea petiolaris* is ideal for a shady wall, with its mass of frothy white flowers in late spring. Only plant these on sound walls, as they can damage old pointing.

Above left **An exuberant skyline is accentuated with abundant planting along every boundary.**
Above **This Parisian garden has seating around the edges to enjoy the spectacular view, and strong but serene planted areas providing a calm haven above the busy city.**

Where you are surrounded on all sides by large buildings, or walls, use the plain background as a way to show off something magnificent. If, for instance, the space is hot and sunny, this is the ideal location for a peach tree, or large fig, or even an evergreen *Magnolia grandiflora*. If the space is more shady and cool, you could grow a lovely silver birch *Betula pendula* in a half barrel.

Sun & shade

Although many urban gardens are small, there is a surprising variation in conditions in them. But it is not as simple as saying, 'south-facing is the sunniest' and 'north-facing is the coolest'.

Effects of light From the point of view of light, an urban garden is more like a clearing in woodland than a garden in farmed countryside. In farmed countryside a garden's aspect is simple: south-facing is hot, north-facing is not. But in the urban environment, a sunny garden can soon become shaded by the growth of the trees around it. On the other hand, a tree that shaded your garden might be felled, turning a once-shady garden into a sun trap. The changes are more subtle than that too: all around the garden, other gardens contain plants that are growing upwards. This is another reason design should be viewed as an organic and on-going process. As a once-sunny wall begins to be shaded by a tree that is shooting up in a neighbour's garden, a fruit tree on it might have to be moved to another wall that is still sunny.

Also, because many urban gardens have tall trees and buildings around them, the sun hits the garden at different times of year in different ways. All this is an argument for getting to know your own garden well, and looking at it to see which areas are sunny, which are hot and dry, which are shady and moist.

For a plant to grow well enough to produce something that is worth eating, it is better to put it in conditions it can thrive in. Lettuces, for example, like cool-dry conditions. In the blazing sun, unless kept well watered all the time, they tend to wilt and bolt, i.e. begin to produce a flower and become bitter. Peaches, on the other hand, adore sun. In shade they may not flower, and if they do, the fruit will not ripen. Chapter 8 details the likes and dislikes of various plants.

Introducing shade However you can use design to alter the conditions in a bed. Where the sun is hot, for instance, you have the opportunity to create multiple layers of greenery. A top layer that can stand blazing sun can grow on a pergola or up wires. This might be a vine, or a fruit tree that is made into a standard, or roses for their scent and colour. Beneath

this can go shrubs or annuals that would not survive full, blazing sun. The base storey could now easily contain lettuces, which will appreciate the dappled shade and the cool. In a small garden, which in the height of summer can become a furnace, dappled shade is both beautiful and delightfully cool.

Another way of creating dappled shade is to plant a tree in your Urban Eden. Many attractive smaller trees cast dappled shade: for example, most of the *Sorbus*, decorative *Acer*, many *Prunus* and the beautiful Snowy Mespilus *Amelanchier canadensis*. Several of the crab apples would serve this function excellently too. *Malus* 'John Downie' is particularly striking,

Below left Contrasts of deep shade and pools of bright light create quite different spaces in a tiny garden.
Below centre Shadows cast by climbing plants around an arched structure cool this dry Mediterranean garden in intense sun.
Below Dappled light filters through layers of edible and ornamental plants climbing over a pergola.

Left At this community garden in east London an interesting ornamental border has been created by weaving apple trees together to maintain all-year interest, from spring blossom to the bare curved stems of winter. *Below left* An enthusiastic gardener with limited space need only leave a path wide enough to walk or wheel a small barrow.

with pink buds, white flowers and attractive orange and scarlet fruits in clusters.

Maximising light Similarly, you can use design to get light into otherwise shady beds. Prune or move surrounding and overhanging plants and a surprising amount of light can be introduced into a bed. Only a few hours of hot sun on a spot can make it suitable for sun-lovers like thyme and rosemary.

Bed Layout

The big advantage of a bed over a container is that it gives a plant access to the soil. That isn't just the soil that is in the bed, it is the soil that extends under walls, under hard landscaping – even under buildings. That's why you can put a large tree or climber in a small bed and have it grow huge.

The traditional wisdom on beds is that they should not be so wide that you cannot work on the back without stepping on them. In a small garden however, you have so little bed space that it really does not matter.

When considering bed layout consider the shadows that are cast across your garden. They will be straight if you are surrounded by buildings. Straight beds integrate well with that. The shadows will be irregular and curved if you are surrounded by trees. Curved beds will blend in better.

It is liberating to design part of a bed which will not have plants in it to allow for sudden inspiration. This is where you put your favourite salad, vegetable or herb. It is fun space where you can play.

Even in a garden with no actual earth – so no actual beds – it is a good design to construct 'beds' out of pots massed together, rather than pots spread about the space. These beds can change as the different plants in the pots come into flower and fruit, and as the sun moves through the sky (see Garden as Gallery, page 80).

Large versus small plants

It is very tempting to fill a small garden with small plants. They are easy to work with, relatively inexpensive to buy, often giving quick results. The trouble with this is that you can soon fill the whole space. Little plants in a little garden look just that – little. As soon as something normal-sized enters the garden, whether this is you, a friend, a passing cat, or even a bird, the whole thing is seen in perspective and can look Lilliputian.

Which is why it is important when designing an Urban Eden to begin by thinking about bigger plants. This is going to be one of the most important design decisions, so think quite hard about it. The rest of the design may well be built and will evolve around one large plant, and, if it is moved, a lot of other plants may have to be moved too.

Above **The wooden raised bed in this garden in Oregon, USA, echoes the formal lines of the verandah behind. The vibrant greenery alongside is reflected in the informal planting.**

Large plants In an Urban Eden, a plant that takes up a lot of room needs to work very hard. If you want to plant a mock orange, for example, look for a small one like *Philadelphus* 'Sybille'. Although the larger-growing *P.* 'Virginal' is a fine shrub, with wonderfully scented flowers, it only flowers for a short period. For the rest of the year it is a fairly anonymous mass of leaf, and it gets to about 2.5m (8ft) high, and quite wide. It takes up too much room for most small gardens. But some plant families work very hard and look very good from early in life: hydrangeas for example are surprisingly tough, able to survive frost in winter, baking heat in summer, direct sun and fairly dense shade. And there are lots of them, in all sorts of colours, with all sorts of leaves. They are deciduous, but flower for a very long time. *Hydrangea serrata* 'Preziosa', for instance, has white lace-cap flowers that turn burnt pink. Its leaf is small and attractive.

One or two large specimens in a small garden, surrounded by smaller plants, with climbers and ground cover, can transform the garden into something dramatic and beautiful. If your garden is sheltered, Californian lilacs *Ceanothus* are good-value large, evergreen shrubs, with intense blue flowers in spring. As they grow, cut the lower branches back and you will quite quickly have a small tree in your garden. Other statuesque plants to consider are the larger *Mahonias*, or the somewhat tender New Zealand flax, *Phormium*.

Trees In a garden devoid of large plants, it makes a lot of sense to introduce a tree into the planting scheme. As with large shrubs, the tree must work hard for its place. It is also worth thinking about how long it will take before it starts to look good. A mature *Acer griseum* has startling peeling bark, and looks great – but it takes five years to get to this stage. That may be too long to wait if you want it to be the design feature around which smaller plants will be placed. Trees that stay small, work hard and look lovely from the start include the crab apples. *Malus laura*, for instance, has lovely pink flowers, and little apples that stay on the tree for a long time and make

superb crab apple jelly. It starts to earn its living very early on in its life. Many birches would work well too. *Betula pendula youngii*, for instance, has a weeping habit, stays fairly small, doesn't bully, has delicate light-green leaves and eye-catching white, or sometimes pink, bark. The coral-barked maple, *Acer senkaki* is a lovely tree which stays small. It's young growth has coral-red bark, so it looks lovely in winter.

Hard landscaping & grass

Be realistic about the location of your hard landscaping. Should it be in the sunniest spot or, in these days of thinning ozone and high-factor sun cream, in a shady one? All too often people put their patio in the sunniest place in the garden, and then have to shelter under a sun canopy when they eat out.

If the area in the middle of your garden is for young kids, grass is an ideal surface. It is safe to fall on, inexpensive to lay, and great to play on. The green of a lawn is also soothing on the eye if you have seen nothing all day but concrete, tarmac and computer screens. However, tiny feet exact a heavy toll on tiny lawns, and the gardener must accept that the small patch of grass is never going to be a bowling green.

But if your main use for the garden will be to entertain friends, you have more choices. Gravel is obviously very easy to put in, though it needs a base. Nowadays there are proprietary fabrics that are specially made for the job (i.e. Terram). They are semi-permeable so they let the water through, but weeds cannot penetrate them. Pack down the subsoil under where the gravel is to go and lay the fabric on the surface, then simply cover with gravel. The fabric stops the gravel and earth mixing when it rains.

Gravel is excellent with curved beds, and comes in a variety of colours. You can also grow plants through it. Against that it is messy, it spreads onto the beds and into the house; cats use it as a huge litter tray; and without a fabric base dandelions and other deep-rooted weeds love it and can be very difficult to eradicate. And very young children find it irresistible for all the wrong reasons: they try to eat it, play football with it, bring

Right In this garden, the hard landscaping of decking, gravel, pebbles and even the furniture is used to create a sense of tranquillity.

Below Allow fragrant herbs such as lavender, oregano and sage to spill out of a mixed border onto a narrow path so that a passer-by cannot avoid brushing the plants and releasing their scent.

Below right Grass paths are best where they are not used too heavily, but they can be very inviting among harder landscaping in an urban space.

it into the house, fall on it and so on! Natural stone, like york and cobbles, is beautiful, obviously incredibly hard-wearing and can be a feature in the garden. However it is expensive and not all that easy to lay.

Brick laid on edge is a good choice for small spaces, ideal beside curved beds. It looks particularly fine with rows of vegetables in potager style. You can incorporate planting holes in the scheme for herbs and flowers and you can be creative with the pattern you choose – but it is time-consuming to lay and you need a good base to work off. If you are covering a large area, or need a very hard-wearing surface, it is worth putting down a proper concrete base of about 7.5cm (3in). Then bed the bricks in a dry 4:1 sand and cement mix about 2.5cm (1in) deep.

Left This border makes the most of rich edible vertical planting with squash and beans clambering up poles and into overhanging trees.
Right The simplest way of adding a permanent vertical element to a small space is to plant one striking golden-leafed robinia.
Above right A fast-growing climber such as scented honeysuckle provides a soft contrast to an industrial-style barrier.

Mosaic can look beautiful, but it requires artistry, patience and time to get right. Wooden decking is light and therefore ideal for roof gardens. It is available ready-made in a number of different styles, and is easy to lay and very attractive. Tannalised softwood is another good choice as it is not too costly and will not rot readily. It is possible to make your own decking, but this is surprisingly time-consuming. The disadvantage of decking is that it can splinter and become very slippery when wet.

Vertical elements

Gardens exist in three dimensions, but many designs seem to do little with the vertical element. In a small garden, where there is limited space, this is especially wasteful. Wherever possible in the Urban Eden, utilise the sky, the earth, and everything in between. In this way you can get much more into even a comparatively small space. Beds should be planted with trees, shrubs and ground cover, but you should also take advantage of all vertical spaces.

Use trees as supports for climbers by tethering ropes or wires in them and growing a climber up into the tree. A honeysuckle like *Lonicera tragophylla* has huge yellow flowers and thrives in the shade of a tree and will never become an overbearing pest.

In most Urban Edens, a pergola can give extra growing space, as well as giving shade under which you can sit. Put it over your sitting area and be surrounded by the scent and blue light of the flowers of a *Wisteria sinensis* in the spring. Use it for beans and roses in the summer. You can even hang fruiting baskets from the horizontal beam. Two fruit trees planted near to each other can be trained into a fruit arch. A row of apple trees trained like this can become a formal walkway, with apples hanging down, offering themselves to be picked as you walk along.

Walls can be covered with hanging baskets on brackets. A spare piece of trellis or mesh can be erected in a bed and used as a climbing frame for squash, or peas, or cucumbers. A wigwam of bamboo stakes can be put in beds to carry climbing beans and sweet peas. Sunny spaces can be crossed by horizontal wires to take vines converting a sun trap into dappled shade, evoking summer scenes in the Mediterranean.

Scent

Scent is one of the most wonderful aspects of an Urban Eden. Living in the city, surrounded by vehicles, spending most of a day in buildings that are filled with warm plastics and heated circuit boards, the scent of a flower in the garden is like a lifeline back to nature.

A pot of sweet peas *Lathyrus odoratus* by the back door, warmed by the sun, heralds the end of a working day, and is sensed even before you step out into the garden. A summer jasmine, *Jasminium officinalis*, placed so that its flowers open by a window or door, will give you a heady burst of pleasure every time you are in the room. Lilies, phlox, pinks, sweet williams, lavender, everyone has their favourites; one of ours is the highly scented *Rosa* 'Guinée', a climber with intense red flowers, and a scent of mango.

Many of the winter-flowering plants have a strong scent. The tiny pink flowers of *Daphne odora* 'Aureomarginata', for instance, are intensely sweet, borne in late winter to early spring. *Viburnum bodnantense* has a beautiful winter scent which lasts for months. Place them so where you will pass them often.

Plant a few clumps of herbs such as sage, marjoram, lavender or mint by paths, or on the edge of a bed so that you release their scent when you brush past them. Many plants also have wonderfully perfumed leaves. Most of the cistus family, in addition to showy flowers, have powerfully aromatic leaves that scent the air around them on a sunny day. Several geraniums have wonderfully scented leaves too and fig leaves have an evocative, 'sticky' smell that envelops the whole tree and the surrounding air when the sun shines on it.

Right A picnic table seen through a lavender hedge. On warm summer evenings when eating out, the scent of lavender drifts over the diners.

Above **Squash, tomatoes, salads, herbs – a striking group of containers filled with plants to eat.**
Above centre **A single, breathtaking specimen, a standard citrus, used on its own as the star of the show.**
Above right **An exquisite pairing: ruby chard in a glazed, green pot.**

And don't forget the plants that will scent the night. A couple of tobacco plants *Nicotiana* growing near where you eat in the garden will subtly perfume the night air, as will night-scented stock *Matthiola*.

Garden as gallery

Plants in containers can be moved about the garden in order to get the best effect throughout the year. For instance, if you have a shrub that flowers brilliantly, like a rhododendron in a

container, it makes sense to bring it into the foreground when it is flowering, and to put it into a bed in the background while it is not. All your flowering and fruiting plants in containers can be treated like this too. Dwarf beans, when they are first in flower and are having their initial crop of beans, look marvellous and can be used as a focal point in the main view. After some weeks bearing beans, however, they tend to lose that fresh perkiness, and can be towards the back, somewhat out of the main view.

If you have an especially decorative pot, it can be used to display a whole succession of beautiful plants in containers. Adam has a particularly lovely big blue ceramic pot. He uses it to display a flowering hellebore *Helleborus orientalis* in late winter which has large, purple-spotted translucent flowers that are best seen from below. In spring it is home to the frothing yellow *Genista lydia*. In summer he uses it to display a pale blue agapanthus, and in late summer a pot of tumbling tomatoes goes into it.

Left These bottles are an ever-changing musical instrument for children. Tap them with a stick and they ring. Changing the level of water in the bottles changes the pitch of the notes.

Below A mirror, placed nonchalantly on a wall, increases the feeling of depth, colour and light in this small garden, without trying to pretend that it is anything other than a mirror.

Below right This metal staircase affords a surprise view.

Beds can be treated in the same way. If you have a good pot of squash growing up bamboos, it can go into a bed to lift a whole area. A sage in a pot could go by a path in summer to scent the area when people brush by it, and on a windowsill in autumn to prevent it getting too wet in winter.

This gallery concept extends to moving plants around the small garden for practical reasons. If a herb in a pot has been overcropped – something that seems to happen a lot to basil – move it out of sight to recuperate for a couple of weeks. When a fruiting plant in a pot is carrying a good crop, move it into the sun to ripen well, or move it into the shade to slow things down. In this way, a small garden can become an ever-changing source of delight.

Surprises

Most of us love surprises, and they can be introduced into even the smallest of gardens. The essence of a surprise, in terms of horticultural design, is that the garden does not present itself to the viewer all at once. Instead, parts are hidden, but are hinted at. The viewer can tell from the design of the garden that there is something just beyond, but has to go there in order to discover what it is. When they arrive, they are delighted.

In a long garden, the way to introduce a surprise is to have a path that snakes off, with a planting placed so that it partially hides the back. The detail of what to plant depends on the style of the garden: with a more formal garden it might be a large, topiarised bay; a Mediterranean garden might have a fig; a more natural garden might have a clump of bamboo left to grow thick.

As for the surprise, the essence of it is that it is unexpected, and welcome. It could simply be a delightful plant, such as a vine covered in bunches of grapes; or a wigwam of squashes; or a fruit archway. It could be a piece of statuary, or a striking pot plant, or a simple water feature. With a water feature, the sound of the water that cannot be seen adds to the anticipation and pleasure.

All-year-round views

It is tempting to have a clear view out from the house across the garden. In practice, this often means a clear view of your back fence or your neighbour's house. So how about borrowing a device from academy painters? Put something tall and fine in the foreground, just in front of the back window. It needs to be something that you can see through. There are many plants that would serve this purpose such as the taller bamboos, which can be thinned to get the perfect degree of screening. The delicate *Cornus contraversa variegata* is lovely, as it forms horizontal layers of pale white and green. Having a plant like this in the foreground will soften your view of the garden. Also, as you move around inside the house looking out, the plant in the foreground will change its position relative to the end of the garden and heighten the sense of perspective, making the garden beyond look bigger.

Another point about views is it is important to think in terms of the whole year. Enthused by good weather, many of us go out to nurseries in the spring and summer, buy plants that are flowering, and plant up our beds so they look great, as viewed from the garden at that moment. This does not take into account that we all spend a great deal of the time inside looking out at the garden, especially during autumn and winter. So when planting in spring and summer plan both for the short term, and for what the garden will look like in late summer, autumn and winter when you are indoors.

Late-flowering plants One of the loveliest flowers in late summer, that will enjoy being under fruit trees, are the various varieties of *Anemone japonica*. The white 'Honorine Jobert' has a superb white flower and is beautiful in the dappled shade of a small fruit tree.

A good winter combination is to contrast delicate flowers with the branches of bare fruit trees. An excellent climber to grow near a spur-pruned apple or pear is the slow-growing winter-flowering clematis *Clematis cirrhosa* 'Balearica' which has pale-pink scented flowers that nod in the slightest breeze. Another lovely combination is a topiarised bay with a pale-green fountain of flowers thrown up by *Helleborus foetidus*.

Topiary

Small gardens often contain bushy shrubs that have become disproportionately big. One way of getting more into your garden and getting more out of it is to clip these so that the bulk of the foliage is held above ground level – in a form of topiary (for examples, see box above). By this we do not mean cutting a large privet into the shape of a chicken; rather, we mean making a neat sculptural shape out of a messy shrub. It might be a cone, or a ball, or – for the ambitious – a corkscrew.

You do not have to be an expert , but watch the flowering period and wait to clip most shrubs after they have flowered. Since you are starting from an established plant, with its own peculiarities, you won't get perfection, at least not at first. The

10 COMMON BUSHY SHRUBS GOOD FOR TOPIARISING

Fuchsia
Myrtle
Camellia
Rhododendron
Forsythia
Pittosporum
Viburnum tinus
Rosemary
Lavender

only way to get an absolutely perfect ball on a dead-straight stem is to grow it with that in mind from an early stage.

Select a shape Look at a shrub that is taking up too much space and try and see if, within, it contains the beginnings of a shape like a column, pyramid, or standard. Then simply clip and tie until you have a rough approximation of that shape. At first it will look a bit loose and rough, but if you keep doing this regularly – depending on its rate of growth, and how neat you want the topiary to be – it will look quite good within a season or two.

Advantages There are many advantages to topiary. You get a formal shape in the garden, which is surprisingly delightful, even – or perhaps especially – in a wild setting. You also learn to appreciate different things about a plant. Many shrubs have beautiful bark on their stems, and turning them into standards exposes this to view (rhododendrons, many fuchsias, hydrangeas). Instead of the shrub obscuring the plants behind it, when you topiarise it you can see round and behind it, so giving you extra perspective which is often hard to achieve in a small garden. Finally, by cutting away the lower growth, you gain extra space all around the shrub for planting new things.

Case Histories

There follow five examples of Urban Edens from a large community garden to the very smallest spaces. These gardens are highly productive and accessible, and give little tasters of what you can achieve in your own garden.

Cameron gardens Until the early eighties, Cameron Gardens was a municipal lawn above an old air-raid shelter. It is situated in the heart of the inner city and boxed in on all sides by buildings. In 1981, Gavin Jones, started to help the local community to turn it into a place where they could grow fresh produce.

The first step, as in many Urban Edens, was to create a raised bed. The central area was raised by almost a metre using a dry-stone wall of slate, and the bed was filled with a potent mixture of leaf-mould, manure and topsoil. Paths were made out of cockle shells, arranged to flow between other separate island beds. The island beds were not raised, but were bordered by box and yew hedging.

In these lower beds Gavin created an fascinating and intricate latticework of trained crab apple trees. When they mature he plans to graft old varieties of apples onto the top of this living sculpture.

The design gives each gardener an area in which to grow what they like. Many grow fascinating edibles. Recently there were tremendous crops of green-skinned, yellow-fleshed pumpkins, with lots of tomatoes as well as masses of coriander. A Bengali plant, *Denki*, is much cultivated for its young shoots which are cooked with fish. The plant, which we call Fat Hen, and which is considered to be a weed in the West, is also cultivated by many of the Bengali gardeners for use in their stews.

Right Overlooked by high buildings, Cameron Gardens is like an oasis for the local residents and wildlife.

The surprise of Cameron Gardens can be anticipated as you round the corner of the bleak housing estate and hear ecstatic birdsong. The framework of the space is made up of an extremely creative use of both plants and recycled materials. The paths which flow between the island beds are made from discarded seashells. The storage shed is made from an upturned trawler. The beds are outlined by an extraordinary mesh of trained crab apple which reflects the design of the wrought-iron gate. The Bengali community gardeners are allocated their own area in which to grow food for their tables.

This organic garden, in the middle of the city, is incredibly productive. In spring and summer it is a cook's paradise. Climbing beans, brassicas and onions mingle with the flowers to make a spectacular display. This is all possible because of the soil, improved by the compost from the four heaps.

Slugs are kept under control by the two much-loved Aylesbury ducks. The pumpkins are supported by empty supermarket orange net bags. This garden has something for everyone and amongst the edibles the children have plenty to play with such as hanging 'musical bottles' filled with water.

Organic garden This is a relatively large garden of 27 x 18m (90 x 60ft) in a fairly busy part of the city. The garden is 18m (60ft) away from the road so there is no threat of lead pollution, particularly as a large building and a wildlife hedge act as barriers between the garden and the cars' exhaust fumes.

The garden has been designed around the needs of Helen's family, and although she describes it as 'short on design and long on organics', she has managed to create a very beautiful space. It is also a very well-run organic garden. Helen never sprays with chemicals and uses companion plantings to attract predators to the pests.

The children have a specific area to run around in where they have a swing and a climbing frame. This robust area in the garden stops the whole from becoming too precious. To sow the seeds of interest, each of the children have their own little plot in which to plant and grow produce. There is also a wildlife pond which the kids adore, full of creepy crawlies.

There is a mixed border in which Helen grows roses and all sorts of herbs including thyme and rosemary. Most of her edibles are grown in three raised beds which are filled with fertile soil, improved by the four compost heaps. Helen's borders are incredibly productive and provide year-round edibles. The compost heaps are used in rotation and have a relatively short maturation period of about four months.

Helen grows masses of salads, brassicas, parsnips and cucumbers as well as some of the more unusual edibles including tomatilloes. Plenty of fruit abounds too, especially apples, pears and soft fruits.

Unusually for a town garden, two ducks are kept as pets. As well as adding a pastoral feel to the garden, they serve the very useful purpose of feeding voraciously on slugs.

This is not just a working garden but a secluded area in which the family can relax away from the hustle and bustle.

City terrace and balcony With such an incredible outside space, these two areas, high above the centre of the city, become the family's main living area in the summer.

With no shade cast by surrounding buildings it can become incredibly hot and is an ideal place to grow Mediterranean fruit and herbs. An automatic irrigation system is a necessity. Even the windy roof terrace grows a spectacular crop of figs and grapes.

Herbs such as rosemary and thyme grow in profusion and scent the balcony with their aromatics. Many summer evening barbecues mean that the herbs are constantly used.

This Urban Eden overlooks an ancient part of the city and is designed with both entertaining and young children in mind.

The banana plants create an exotic decoration in the summer. In this garden where there are no beds, every planting space is used to the full: even the banana is underplanted.

Unusual combinations, such as a pear with the New Zealand flax are incredibly striking.

The barbecue and herb area (above) is adjacent to the kitchen, making it very easy to pluck a few herb leaves whether cooking indoors or out.

In Adam's garden, sunshine is at a premium. To get the best-tasting herbs, and to use the sunshine above the beds that was not being exploited, he hung a herb basket from a scaffolding pole up which he grew a vine.

For maximum use of space in this bed herbs colonise the bottom storey, flowering and fruiting medium-sized plants above, and trees form the background and upper layer. Runner beans, beautiful edibles.

Ornamentals such as clematis could not be denied a place in even a largely edible garden.

Above Adam turned a clearing under a tree into a surreal jungle glade with this tree-fern in a glazed turquoise pot.

Adam's garden is fairly small, 5 x 15m (16 x 50ft), and is surrounded by mature trees in other gardens, so he originally designed it to reinforce the feeling of being in a woodland. At the back he planted a group of trees: *Eucalyptus gunnii* (silver-grey foliage and ribbons of peeling bark); sumach *Rhus typhina* (a dome-shaped spreading tree with fiery red and yellow leaves in autumn); and *Robinia pseudacacia frisia* (a bright golden-leafed tree). The fence on one side was ramshackle pallisades, which he planted shrubs against; the wall on the other side was obscured largely by a *Buddleja davidii* planted in a neighbouring garden. The garden had a rather wonderful, wild feeling.

Then Adam decided that he wanted to transform this into an Urban Eden without losing the woodland feel. The first priority was to free up space. The *Buddleja* was pruned back – but not so that its screening effect was lost. This gave much more light and bed space, but revealed more of the unattractive wall, which Adam painted green.

Two unruly pittosporums and a bay tree had taken over a large proportion of the bed space. These were clipped into balls, one at ground level, two into high standards. Underneath them he planted fennel and garlic chives. By the pond a shrubby myrtle *Myrtus tarentina* was also standardised. Because its habit is slightly weeping, and its trunk is bent, it looks ancient, mysterious and magical.

There was an established bed structure of straight, slightly raised beds. In these Adam planted tumbling nasturtiums, thyme and mint. Plants with all-year-round interest were placed where they could be seen from the house: both the Christmas and the Easter rose, *Helleborus orientalis* and *Helleborus niger*. These flourish in the semi-shade, and flower with strange, unworldly green blooms in the winter and early spring respectively. An *Akebia quinata*, a climber that has chocolate-purple flowers in early spring, was planted to climb up the eucalyptus.

With more light in the bed near the house, pots were planted full of tomatoes. Adam filled a big old terracotta pot with French beans surrounded by Lollo Rosso lettuce.

Rosemary Severn Sea covers the ground just by a group of box, while in the bed sits a large Ali Baba pot in which is a purple-leafed *Pittosporum* 'Tom Thumb'. Behind this he planted another fennel, its feathery yellow flowers contrasting beautifully with the purple of the pittosporum. As one of many surprises in the garden, Adam has put a pot of squash in a container sculpted out of the remnants of an old wall. Further towards the back is a raised bed on which he has planted blackberries and courgettes.

To exploit the vertical element wires have been strung into trees to take runner beans, and baskets full of strawberries and herbs hang from trees like some weird fruit. Tumbling tomatoes are used as a decorative border around the pond with a collection of other herbs.

The feeling in the garden has changed. Where before it was mysterious, and a little forbidding, it has become welcoming, cheerful and productive.

James's garden When James and his family moved into their current house, the garden was a shabby little area 6m (20ft) square of paving with almost no plants in it and two big tree stumps in the corners.

The walls of the garden were low. If they were built-up to give privacy the views of the distant trees would have been lost, and the garden would have become claustrophobic. So instead trellis was put on top of the walls. It provided screening, and an additional vertical growing surface.

The principal eyesore was the buildings opposite, so to distract from them two fig trees were planted behind the tree stumps at each corner of the garden. These would provide interest in the summer with their exotic, curvaceous leaves, fruit and even winter interest with their grey bark. The figs were planted level with the top of the walls, in beds built up behind the stumps and in the angle of the walls. In this way, they would quickly overhang the tree-stump chairs, and their leaves would top the trellis within a couple of years. The low walls were painted white to brighten the whole garden.

The centre of the garden was paved, and slightly raised straight beds were built along each wall. Fruit trees on dwarf rootstock were planted in the middle of each bed on both sunny walls. They break the strong lines of wall and trellis, and promise a delicious crop. A white-fleshed peach Amsden June was chosen for one wall, and a greengage Cambridge Gage was put against the other. Both trees are being loosely fan-trained.

In order to introduce the element of surprise the tree stumps were not left plain, but were sculpted into a pair of wooden armchairs, one of which is button-backed.

This garden is so tiny that it is essential for the vertical element to be fully exploited. Horizontal arms were added to the trellis post uprights, extending out over the beds. Straining wires were threaded through them, creating a canopy above each bed. Straining wires were also put along the walls. Climbing roses have burst through the canopy, which supports runner beans and a vine Leon Millot in summer.

The bed facing the house is reserved for flowering plants only. The bulk of the beds on the left and right are left for planting whatever summer crop takes the family's fancy. Currently the sunnier of these contains garlic, copious wild rocket plants, a new crop of rocket as replacement, garlic chives, rosemary, golden oregano, thyme and ordinary chives, with alpine strawberries flowing over the edge of the beds. The shadier one contains leaf celery, fennel, sorrel and spinach.

Topiary has helped to get more into the garden. A pair of *Fuchsia magellanica* 'Alba' has been turned into standards. With their papery barked trunks, and their untidy heads bearing little white flowers that look like earrings, they are a stunning feature.

The whole design continues to evolve. In the hot sun of midsummer, the family have discovered that the garden is too hot to sit in, so the vine is being trained in the air across the space. The garden no longer looks shabby and derelict. It now hums with activity and interest.

Even though James's garden is small, because the trellis is open it does not feel confined. The mixture of fruit trees, vegetables, salads, herbs and ornamental plants gives it a robust feeling, and an interesting look for almost the whole year. Because it is a well-used garden, it cannot afford to be too manicured.

Although there are always plenty of small jobs to do, if life gets busy and the garden cannot be tended for some time, it tends to look after itself. This is at least partly due to the fact that James uses no chemicals but follows organic principles, a practice which pays off even when gardening in a small urban space.

5 Slugs & snails · Toads & frogs · Earthworms · Aphids · Hoverflies, lacewings & ladybirds · Bees & wasps
Caterpillars · Spiders · Other insects · Vine weevils · Birds · Cats

guide to urban wildlife

An Urban Eden gives you the opportunity to enjoy organic food for almost no cost because the mix of ornamentals and edibles creates ideal conditions for growing food without chemicals. The blooms of the ornamental plants attract beneficial insects, and because plants in an Urban Eden are all grown in with each other, rather than in big groups, pests and diseases are unlikely to spread widely.

Organic gardening in the urban environment also makes a significant ecological impact to the wider environment because our towns and cities have become an important reservoir of wildlife. Far from being the deserts many consider them to be, they contain more habitats than much of today's countryside, and these habitats are in general less subject to being sprayed with chemicals that harm wildlife. Urban honeys often win prizes in honey-tasting competitions because the bees in cities have a much wider range of flowers to feed on than their country cousins. And what is true for bees, is true for other insects.

This needn't mean that the Urban Eden is a paradise for pests. By knowing more about which creatures are allies and which are foes, and how to assist the allies and limit the damage from the foes, your garden can be as well-kept as any.

You may find yourself becoming fascinated by the lives that share your garden, adding an extra dimension of interest to your gardening.

There is one general rule about creepy-crawlies in the garden. The ones that move fast are usually friends; the ones that move slowly are enemies. That's because the fast-moving ones are carnivores, using their speed to catch their prey. The slow-moving ones tend to be herbivores and they don't need to expend energy dashing about. So snails, slugs and aphids are bad news; spiders, wasps and bees good.

This rule of thumb comes into its own when you find something you've never come across before. If a large unrecognised beetle scuttles off quickly, it's likely to be a friend. If it plods around slowly, it is probably a foe. But there are exceptions to every rule – ladybird larvae, for example, don't move fast but they have a sensational appetite for aphids and are a gardener's important allies. This is where a certain amount of knowledge helps.

Best method of pest control Pest predators are more effective than any other form of control: when hungry ladybird larvae have eaten all the aphids on one plant, they seek out the next infested plant and eat all the aphids there too, they grab any that hatch out of eggs and also eat any that fly onto your plants. Unlike sprays, a pest's natural enemies are completely specific for whatever they target, have no side effects, keep working, and move about, seeking their targets.

Contrast that with spraying with a broad-spectrum insecticide. The first application kills lots of aphids, but also lots of predators. As soon as the chemical has ceased to be effective, the aphids return faster than the predators, whose numbers take much longer to build up. So once you start spraying, you become dependent on it.

Plant health The most effective defence against pest attack is to ensure that your plants are well nurtured. A strong, healthy plant is much better able to endure or even resist

attack. Plants have complex defences that we are only just beginning to understand, including production of chemicals to deter insects trying to eat them, and chemicals to alert surrounding plants that these attacks have begun.

Finally, because you are not going to starve if a crop fails, cultivate a bit of tolerance for the other lives that share the garden. If an apple has a spot or two, or a lettuce leaf has been partly munched, it won't taste any different.

Slugs & snails

Some species of slug are tiny, others as big as an adult's thumb. They vary from cream to black through vivid oranges, and most are voracious herbivores. Dozens of snail species also infest gardens, all of which are hugely destructive. Both are particularly active in spring and during moist spells in summer

when they chomp away at the softest parts of plants, the growing tips, young seedlings and new leaves.

Methods of control Don't try to control slugs and snails with conventional slug pellets, as these are very harmful to birds too. Wildlife veterinarians report horrific injuries to birds whose stomachs have been destroyed after eating slug pellets, or eating slugs that have eaten slug pellets. And even in a garden that is heavily pelleted, there will still be lots of slugs and snails.

The organic way of dealing with them is to wage a war of attrition. The fact that most Urban Edens are small is an advantage here. Start with a blitz. Eliminate every slug and snail you find by throwing them against a hard surface, or collecting them in a bag and dropping them into the nearest pond (ducks love snails and slugs). Inspect their hiding places daily – they shelter anywhere cool and shady, especially if it is also moist. Look under stones and pots, in the cracks of walls, on the bed-side of ornamental edging and beneath large-leafed plants and favourites like hostas and ivy. Occasional early-morning or evening slug hunts are also effective; at night, a torch will pick out their slime trails, making this a particularly rewarding time to hunt.

Some organic gardeners also use beer traps, containers of beer sunk into the soil around vegetables. Slug pellets made of aluminium sulphate are harmless to other wildlife, although they are only effective till it rains. Another control is nematodes (tiny worms which eat slugs). These are supplied

Left Slugs are one of the chief irritants to a gardener, adoring young leafy greens and most vegetables. Hostas are another favourite snack and even application of pellets does not guarantee to keep your precious plants safe.

Right These young tomato plants are being protected from slug and snail attack by a section cut from a plastic bottle. This also provides them with a sheltered micro-climate. These modern cloches have their own contemporary, urban charm.

Above **Even when frogs are not going about the business of consuming slugs and snails, they are wonderful to watch.**

in a powder and are watered onto beds once the soil has warmed up. The nematodes will kill slugs for up to a couple of months as long as the soil remains moist and the weather warm for that period.

Where slugs and snails are a major problem, start plants from seed in spring in pots away from beds. Grow these seedlings on in pots until they are big enough to be less vulnerable. Precious specimens can be temporarily protected in a bed with a barrier of sharp sand, though this will only last until the sand is washed away. A plastic sleeve (cut from a clear plastic drink bottle) put over a young plant will also give temporary protection.

Toads & frogs

Frogs and toads eat large quantities of slugs and snails and are a fascinating addition to any Urban Eden. They are entertaining to watch, and irresistible to young children. All they require is some still water in which to breed.

So, if you have the space, build a small pond, ideally with gently sloping sides. Get spawn in spring from another garden pond. Unlikely as this seems to those who have never tried it, when you ask around you should soon discover a source. Frog spawn is round and comes in clumps; toad spawn comes in strings.

The main enemies of toads and frogs in the urban environment are cats, slug pellets and herbicides. Many pond fish also eat the tadpoles. In winter, both frogs and toads hibernate, often under logs, which is one more excuse not to tidy up the garden excessively!

Earthworms

Earthworms should be encouraged in your garden. There are many species, almost all of which are beneficial. Their burrowing improves soil aeration and drainage, and as they move around they feed on plant litter and its by-products, excreting it as 'casts' of a soil-like substance that feeds the soil.

With a healthy earthworm population, the soil becomes light, crumbly, rich and open. Without earthworm activity, soil tends to compact and plants' roots will suffer. In New Zealand, where there are few native beneficial earthworms but a voracious carnivorous earthworm, the New Zealand flat worm, in places where beneficial earthworms have been introduced there are large increases in crop yields.

To increase the earthworm population in an Urban Eden you need to provide them with lots of compost and manure as food. If you feed your soil regularly with organic matter, worms will flourish. You can lay compost and manure on the surface for the worms to drag under, or dig it in.

Many commonly used pesticides can kill worms. This is another potent argument for keeping organic. A healthy earthworm population will also provide food for many birds.

Aphids

Most of the world's 4,400 aphids live on specific host plants and are not pests. But a few live on a wide variety of plants, and breed astonishingly quickly, and it is these that cause the problems. They include the greenfly, blackfly and whitefly.

They harm plants directly by sucking out their sap, and indirectly by introducing virus diseases and by producing honeydew on which sooty moulds develop. These sooty moulds clog up the pores of leaves, thereby reducing their ability to photosynthesise.

Luckily, aphids have many predators. Ladybirds, hoverflies and lacewings live off them, and some spiders and beetles include aphids in their diet. Once the predator populations build up, a garden can be relatively clear of aphids with no help from you. Sadly, however, aphids get going earlier in the year than most of their enemies which can result in a huge population of aphids that can be difficult to eradicate.

At the start of the season do all you can to get rid of aphids and preserve the predator population. If you only have a few plants, just squash the aphids between your fingers. With more plants, you can kill aphids with soapy water because they have a waxy exterior which dissolves in soap. Horticultural soap is most effective, but any soapy water has some effect.

Right **If predators do not get control of a prey population in time, an infestation may get so severe that you have to interfere and use other methods of reducing their impact. To combat aphid infestations without resorting to chemicals, squish as many bugs as possible before spraying any affected plants with a soapy water mixture as often as you need.**

Above **Once you start to notice bees, there is a whole world of them to be discovered: different shapes, sizes, colours and habits. All are useful to pollinate your plants.**

Once the predators arrive, stop using any other pest control and let a balance get established between aphids and predators. It takes a bit of time, and requires courage – some plants will look shabby for a short period while predator populations grow – but then the aphids will start to disappear.

Do all you can to avoid chemical sprays. Although they are very effective in the short term, they also kill the aphid's predators. And whereas aphids can hide in leaf sheaths, and multiply speedily from just a few survivors, predator populations are slower to recover. So once you start spraying, you have to continue or suffer continued, permanent population explosions of aphids. And try to avoid using chemicals on plants you are going to eat.

Some 'green' sprays are widely available, and although these are preferable to out-and-out pesticides, even these are not always safe for the predator populations.

Hoverflies, lacewings & ladybirds

Hoverflies Hoverflies look like slimline flat-bodied bees and wasps, but hover like little helicopters. There are many species of hoverfly, and they all have the great virtue that their larvae eat aphids, with the adults laying their eggs directly into aphid colonies. So you definitely want to encourage them into your garden. They like open-faced flowers such as marigolds rather than flowers with deep trumpets.

Lacewings Like hoverflies, you may never have consciously seen lacewings. Their name is apt as they have elegant diaphanous wings. Their larvae look like miniature alligators, and eat aphids. They are attracted by most garden flowers.

Ladybirds It seems that everyone likes ladybirds. There are all sorts, with different numbers of spots, and even with different-coloured bodies. They look charming, they eat aphids, and their larvae are champion aphid destroyers; a ladybird larva is a small, tapering, segmented creature that looks rather like a tiny armadillo with pale-pink spots on its body, which you may see in spring.

Bees & wasps

Bees are a vital link in the ecological chain that supports us all as they pollinate flowers. There are lots of varieties, from tiny ones to large bumblebees, from social ones to solitary ones. In order to attract them into the garden all you need are lots of flowering plants; some species such as Bee Balm Monarda, and most flowering herbs and heavily fragrant flowers such as lavender are real bee magnets. Like other

insects, bees can be harmed by careless use of insecticides. They will only sting as a last resort so if you don't disturb them, they will leave you alone.

Wasps are the gardener's friends too. They are carnivores, devouring pests like aphids and caterpillars. They can become something of a nuisance in late summer as they raid ripe fruit, particularly plums and greengages, but for most of the summer they quietly get on with their business of patrolling flowering plants. Wasps sting more readily than bees, but again, only when protecting themselves.

Caterpillars

It used to be so simple: caterpillars ate plants, therefore they were bad, so they were killed. But the sad truth is, no caterpillars, no butterflies, and butterflies and moths are becoming increasingly rare.

Most caterpillars are specific to certain species of plants. In general, these aren't the pests. So, unless your plants are hit by masses of caterpillars (and some species do appear in huge numbers locally), leave them.

But there are also some pest species, those caterpillars that are not choosy about what plants they eat, or those that destroy whole plant populations. The caterpillars of the large cabbage white are yellow and black and hairy; the caterpillars of the small cabbage white are yellowish green and not very hairy. Pick them off by hand and throw them onto a hard surface, or drop them into a slug beer trap.

You may find caterpillars in winter as well as spring, since some live through the winter, becoming butterflies or moths in the next summer.

Spiders

Spiders are all friends of the gardener. Recent research has established that plants visited by spiders produced more seeds than ones that were not visited by spiders. The explanation is that spiders hunt and eat the pests that harm plants. There are dozens of species of spider in the garden and the more you get to know them, the more you'll see. Even in northern European gardens you come across dozens of species, including the common garden spider which makes a web; the wolf spider which runs about carrying its eggs on its back; jumping spiders which live on walls; diadem spiders with beautifully marked bodies, and numerous others.

All spiders are carnivorous, immobilising their prey by injecting them with venom. Most are territorial, which means that once you've spotted one, you will see it again and again through the year. They are busy and persistent, and have interesting habits: they hunt, quiver with anticipation of a kill, wrap things they have caught in silk, repair their webs (if they make them)… and so on.

We recently found a whole community of tiny spiders making webs and catching aphids; it was a lovely sight.

Other insects

Ants aerate the soil, which is good, but unfortunately they also protect and spread aphids. If you watch a plant that has aphids on it, you may see ants hurrying up and down the plant. They are actually 'farming' the aphids, collecting the aphids' honeydew, and also protecting them from predators. If you get on top of the aphid problem, you can leave the ants alone.

Woodlice mostly eat decomposing matter, so are no great threat to gardens unless their numbers build up. A large woodlice population can damage seedlings and young plants, so remove any rotten wood and piles of dead leaves where they flourish.

Beetles Most beetles in the domestic garden are fast-moving and are efficient predators of many pests. They can be encouraged by providing them with places to hide such as leaves on the soil, or dense planting. Centipedes and millipedes do little harm.

Vine weevils

The vine weevil is a slow-moving beetle and a terrible pest. The adult is a small, greyish-black beetle with a slow gait, but vine weevils are excellent walkers and can even climb skyscrapers. If you see a leaf with what looks like slits cut into it a vine weevil has been at work. Kill them on sight.

An adult can lay more than 1,000 eggs in one go and the larvae do the serious harm, devouring roots. They are small U-shaped white grubs that reach 1 cm ($\frac{1}{2}$ in) in length and can eat virtually the whole of a plant's rooting system before you know that they are present. Generally you only discover them when a plant won't thrive in spite of everything that is done by way of feeding and watering. One day you touch its stem and discover that it is loose in the earth, and when you dig it up you will find just a few roots left, and scores of fat white grubs in the soil.

Control Vine weevils used to be controlled with chemicals, but these were widely harmful and withdrawn from the market. New composts are available which contain insecticide but these aren't suitable for edible crops. Some biological controls target vine weevils but these are generally only suitable for controlled environments.

If you are in an area that is subject to vine weevil attack, the best way to protect your plants is through very careful management. Never recycle compost from pots from year to year. Do not put primulas, polyanthus, cyclamen or busy lizzies *Impatiens* into beds or mixed plantings with edibles as vine weevils love all of these. However, these same plants are useful as traps. Pot them up in a compost that contains imidacloprid and place them around the garden. Simply destroy these trap plants at the end of summer.

If you do find vine weevils in a containerised plant, and the damage is not too great, remove all the soil from the plant's roots, and replace it with new. The soil from the plant needs to be thrown out with the domestic rubbish as it is likely to contain innumerable vine weevil eggs.

Above **Spiders are territorial and build their webs in the same place time and again. Once you get to know an individual, you can watch them grow and change and develop.**

Birds

Once, because finches pecked at the flower buds on fruit trees, and crops of soft fruit were decimated by birds, they were considered something of a pest. But in fact, birds are a great help in the garden, consuming large quantities of slugs, snails and caterpillars. Unfortunately, bird numbers have declined disastrously in many places recently, for a variety of reasons, including increased use of chemicals in urban gardens.

Attracting birds To encourage more birds in the garden – and for most city dwellers it is a delight to have a bird keep you company when you garden, waiting for you to turn up soil and reveal juicy tit-bits – there are several courses of action. Reduce the hunting success of pet cats by putting a bell on them. Never use snail and slug pellets. Grow a few bushy shrubs in which birds can nest. Also, it helps birds greatly if you don't neaten things up too much in the garden in autumn. A few dried rose hips left on unpruned bushes, a few seed-heads on the rudbeckia, leaves on the beds to attract earthworms to the surface – all these help birds overwinter.

If you want to go a bit further, you can take the positive steps of growing plants in which birds can nest safely. They like a bit of cover, something overgrown and dense and bushy. Pyracantha, a plant that has fallen out of favour with trendy designers, is great, especially if it is left to get a bit wild.

Cats

Cats are a fact of urban life. They defecate away from their home, which means in someone else's garden. So, if there are lots of cats in your area, your garden can reek, and you have to fight a battle constantly and tenaciously to get rid of the problem.

First, a short digression on cat behaviour. Cats select an area in which to defecate, and then go there repeatedly. They seem to particularly like newly turned soil. Once they start using an area, they keep on going there, locating their spot by smell.

Clearing your garden of cats The first step is to clean up all excrement and the tainted soil under it thoroughly to remove the smell. Wrap it in newspaper, bag it up and dispose of it with the domestic rubbish. Then turn the soil, so that there is no trace of cat smell left. If available, add plentiful organic matter to hide the smell further. Then water it thoroughly to leach away anything unpleasant that may still be lingering in the soil.

You now have to ensure that the area is not reclaimed. There are various chemical compounds on the market that can be spread in this area which work well – that is, until it rains. Holly and rose clippings deter cats too. But with determined cats, even these can be ignored. There is another solution. Once the ground is clean and smells fresh, sink 15cm (6in) lengths of stake or branches of wood into the ground at 10cm (4in) intervals with half protruding above ground. These stakes make it physically difficult for the cats to squat. This is the feline equivalent of anti-tank defences.

What happens now is that the cats will go to the nearest undefended area and defecate there. Simply clean this up, and extend the defences. Soon the local cats will just have to go elsewhere, a new toilet will be established, and the problem is permanently solved.

With a particularly valuable newly planted specimen, or with particularly determined cats, you may have to go one step further and fix chicken wire to the stakes above ground. This is totally effective. Once the specimen is established, you can remove the chicken wire.

6

Spring · Summer · Autumn · Winter

the urban eden cycle

In the old days there was, as the song says, a time for sowing and a time for reaping. Modern horticulture has done what it can to make all that irrelevant. Increasingly, you can buy seedlings and kindergarten plants that take away the need to sow. And new early- and late-cropping varieties mean that the time for reaping has been extended from very early spring to late winter.

It is now also possible to avoid doing some of the other gardening chores that used to have to be done at certain times of year. Dwarf rootstocks, for instance, have taken much of the urgency out of pruning. Container-grown plants can be planted out virtually any time of year except, for obvious physical reasons, when frost and snow freeze the ground. Plants have been developed with disease resistance, and this has reduced some of the pressing need for spraying and painting and clearing.

That said, there are still seasonal jobs, and still tips that the Urban Eden gardener should know to be able to get the best out of the garden. And doing garden tasks at the appropriate time of year is part of getting back into rhythm with the natural cycle of seasons.

Spring

Seed sowing The key to successful sowing is to follow the instructions on the back of seed packets faithfully. If you aren't familiar with certain words and concepts, these instructions can be quite difficult to interpret. This is the Urban Eden guide to deciphering the language of seed packets.

Sow in spring Spring is a moveable feast. It means the time of year when young seedlings can go outside without having to endure a hard frost. It's a bit of a lottery, with each gardener making a personal judgement about precisely when that is. If a packet says 'sow in early spring' it means the seeds can stand a bit of frost, and you can sow outside a bit earlier.

Plants take a certain amount of time to germinate, grow, mature and be ready for eating. If you wait to sow until too late they may not have time to complete their cycle. Also, early crops are particularly desirable: once the season for something is in full swing, it rapidly loses its rarity value. Experienced gardeners often take a chance and sow a few seeds outside quite early and, if they are killed by a late frost, sow a few more after the frost.

Another strategy is to sow indoors. This protects the young plants from the frost, and gives them a head start, particularly valuable for rather tender plants such as tomatoes, peppers, sweetcorn and cucumber. Once all danger of frost is past, you have strong seedlings to plant out. You don't need a greenhouse for this: a bright window will do.

However, indoor-grown plants need to be 'hardened off' before they can be planted out successfully. Put them outside in a sheltered spot in their growing containers before going into the soil. For the first few nights you may have to take them in to a cool place if it looks like there might be frost. After a week or two you can plant them out in a bed and leave them to fend for themselves.

One way of planting seedlings out a little early is to protect them with a cloche, either traditional glass or simply polythene on wire hoops. Victorian-style bell-jars are the ornamental alternative to a large clear plastic bottle which does the same job for individual plants. However, with sun shining on it a cloche can be a death trap for a seedling as the temperature inside soars, so open cloches or remove them entirely on sunny days.

Hundreds of seeds Many seed packets contain enough seeds to fill a small garden completely, enough to supply an entire street, let alone a family, so there are usually plenty left over after you've sown what you want.

Inside the outer paper seed packet there is often a little airtight metal foil packet which contains the actual seeds. Open this foil packet carefully and scatter a few seeds where you want them, then fold over and reseal the foil packet and pop it back, immediately, into the paper presentation packet. Immediately is important – if you don't get the right foil packet into the right paper pack, it is all too easy to end up with half a dozen resealed foil packets, and no idea which is which.

If one year you find that the seeds don't germinate, they're past their use-by date.

Succession sowing This is the practice of sowing your first batch of plants early, then sowing more later so that you have crops through the summer.

Planting in a seed tray or pot If you are planting in a pot to transplant out later, it is best to disturb the seedling's root as little as possible. So you don't want to plant the seed in a huge depth of soil, and have to chase the end of the root down inches to get it out. You put only about 3–4cm (1–2in) of seed compost into a seed tray, which means the roots don't go too deep. When you transplant them, the seedlings aren't set back too much. A simple propagator – a seed tray with a clear plastic top – is a great help.

Or you can sow into an 8cm (3in) pot – nothing smaller as a very small volume of compost dries out very quickly. If you use an old pot, wash it out first; it's like a baby's bottle, it's best

Right **Most people find sowing seeds both nerve-racking and exciting. However many times you experience it, it still seems a miracle when they germinate and race up towards the light. Although seedlings should be treated tenderly, they are often less fragile and more adaptable than they appear.**

to be hygienic around newborns, even though they might be able to survive a bit of infection.

Seed compost If you want your seeds to have the best start use seed compost rather than any old soil. It has a fine structure, so is easily penetrated by the seedling's root and shoot. It is sterile, so the seeds won't get attacked by diseases, or any pest that is lurking in the soil. It is also low in nutrients; seedlings can 'burn' easily if the compost is too rich.

Moist compost One of the commonest causes of seedlings dying is 'damping off'. This is not too little water, but too much. If the soil in which the seedlings are growing is constantly wet, they just get soggy and die. You need to get the compost moist but not wet. It is best to water it and leave it to drain for an hour or two before you sow the seeds. Then spray the pot regularly.

Nor should compost be allowed to get bone dry. To check, lift your pot and feel its weight. If it is feels light, it's too dry so plunge it in a bowl of water for a few minutes till the compost is wet again and then let it drain.

Fine tilth This means that the surface of the soil, your seedbed, should be made very fine. This is necessary as it ensures that there are no big lumps of earth which could impede the seedlings' roots and, as a result, its growth. Create a fine tilth by chopping the topsoil lightly with the edge of a trowel.

Sow in rows/drills a certain distance apart A drill is a little furrow in which seeds are planted in vegetable gardens or allotments. The relevance to an Urban Eden gardener is that it tells you the right spacing of the plants.

Thin You need to take out small plants in a crowded group of seedlings in order to give the ones that remain enough room to grow. However, if you begin by sowing your seeds quite carefully, you may not have to thin them out later. If you have to thin, carefully pull up the weakest plants – in the case of salads and green leafy vegetables such as spinach and chard, instead of adding them to your compost bin, why not use them in a salad? Try to disturb the roots of the remaining plants as little as possible.

Left **As plants grow larger through the summer, crop them regularly to keep them producing strong foliage. Keeping them relatively compact also cuts down on the amount of water they need.**

Right **Plants grown in containers always need more watering than those grown in open ground, but all plants need regular watering as the year warms up.**

Label the pots Although it is easy to remember which seed is in which pot when you sow them, three or four weeks later it can be quite confusing. One year, for instance, we got very enthusiastic about chillies and sowed a whole lot of different Californian seeds without labelling the pots other than 'chillies'.

Only one lot of seedlings did well. In fact, it did fantastically, resulting in loads of little chilli plants to give away. Except when they appeared they weren't chillies, they were weird balls of green encased in a papery covering. After some research, it was established that these plants were in fact Green Husk tomatillos. Which was a relief: at least they were edible! If the pot had been labelled properly, a lot of trouble would have been avoided.

Label each pot with its contents and date of sowing.

Transplanting If you sow seeds indoors, or in a seed pot or tray, at some stage you have to transplant them out into the garden. The trick is to do it at the right time. Leave seedlings until they are big enough to handle, but do not allow them to get so big that their growth is stunted by their being crowded. The ideal moment is when they have at least four leaves and are quite sturdy. Hold the seedlings by their leaves to transplant them, stick a pencil into the compost and gently lever out the roots.

Don't plant seedlings out too soon or you might lose the plants to an unexpected frost. And watch out for slugs and snails – a good short-term Urban Eden fix is to cut the top and bottom off a big plastic bottle and sink it over the most precious seedlings. It isn't foolproof, but it does offer some protection from predators.

Planting out/crop rotation Crops are rotated around the dedicated vegetable garden or allotment because every plant takes up specific minerals and nutrients from the soil. If the same vegetables are grown in the same spot year after year, some of those nutrients can become depleted even if the soil is regularly improved. At the same time, the pests and diseases that target a particular plant can build up in the soil year on year.

In the Urban Eden, where vegetables and ornamentals are grown together, you don't need to follow any particular rotation scheme. Just avoid growing exactly the same plants in the same position every year. If members of the *Brassica* family (cabbage, broccoli, cauliflower etc.) are grown in the same place two years running, then club root, a soil-borne fungal disease, can quickly build up in the soil. If an old fruit tree needs to be replaced, simply choose a tree that bears a different type of fruit.

Mulching It's a good idea to mulch the soil to conserve moisture in a hot summer. A mulch is a thick layer of organic matter simply laid on the soil's surface. It protects the top of the bed from the direct rays of the sun without itself holding water. When you water, the liquid goes straight through the top protective layer and is then absorbed by the topsoil. Because that doesn't get heated by the sun, the water doesn't evaporate so quickly.

Always mulch when the soil is wet. If you mulch dry soil, it can get really parched under the mulch, and when you water it will all disappear down the cracks, failing to wet the soil. You'll only notice what is happening when plants start to die.

A rainwater barrel is a good idea, a good fall-back supply in hot summers. Unfortunately, of course, in drought the barrel won't be refilled as it is drained, so won't last that long. But even a few days grace might get your garden over a water crisis. To stop the water in a rainwater barrel becoming

Summer

Summer is the time when plants grow most rapidly. It is also the time when things can easily go wrong, particularly with watering.

Watering The temptation during hot spells is to give the garden a quick spray in the morning, as if to see it through the day. Although this is better than not watering at all, a quick spray only wets the top of the soil. This encourages plant roots to stay on the surface, thus increasing their vulnerability to drought because it is this top layer of soil that dries first in hot weather. Also, most of the water you spray on the soil like this evaporates in the heat of the day before the plants can take it up.

It is much more effective to water thoroughly at the end of the day. As everything cools down, give the garden a good soaking. This encourages deep rooting, and gives the plants all night to take up the water.

fetid, you must clean it out once a year, and place some crushed charcoal in the bottom of it to help to keep the water sweet for longer.

Plants can also be watered by so-called 'greywater', water that has been used for bathing and washing. However, greywater should never be used on edible plants except fruit trees, because of the tiny particles of waste matter and detergents it contains.

Feeding If your soil is healthy and gets regular infusions of composted organic matter and manure, everything in the Urban Eden will flourish. However, you sometimes need to add extra feed, particularly when growing plants in containers. If you do this, it is important to match the right feed to the crop in question.

There are three nutrients that plants need in fairly large quantities: nitrogen (N), phosphorus (P) and potassium (K). Crudely, nitrogen promotes vigorous leaf growth, phosphates promote root growth, and potassium encourages flowering and fruiting. So if you want more of a leaf crop, apply a high-nitrogen feed. However, put that on a tomato and you'll get lots of leaves and stem – but not more or better tomatoes. For a tomato – or for other fruiting crops – a high potassium feed is much better.

Feeds that promise miraculous extra growth tend to be very high in nitrogen. One problem is that although high nitrogen will make the garden look green and lush, and give you large vegetables, crops produced this way tend to taste watery. Herbs fed nitrogen lose a large part of their tang. The other problem is that large, juicy, soft, sappy nitrogen-pumped leaves and stems seem to be irresistible to aphids and other sucking insects.

Summer pruning If a fruit tree is left completely unpruned for too many years, the risk arises of biennial cropping. What happens is that the tree bears a heavier and heavier crop until one year the crop is so large that the tree gets exhausted.

As a result, the next year it will bear no crop. During this rest year it grows well and recovers, ready to bear another huge crop the following year (of usually small fruit). This huge crop exhausts the tree once again, and the biennial pattern is established.

To avoid this, in a year where the tree is carrying a very heavy crop, remove fruit before it ripens so that the tree bears only its usual load. And prune it lightly in summer to encourage it to flower the following year. The rule here is to think about the wood on which it flowers. Apples and pears flower on short spurs of old wood, so when pruning to encourage next year's flowers, cut new long growths back to only three or four buds. Peaches and other stone fruit flower only on last year's growth, so cut out a few of the stems that bore fruit this year.

Autumn

The first job of autumn is to prepare the compost area for an influx of new material. If you have timed everything right, the compost bin should contain well-rotted compost, and perhaps a stout plastic bag or two of somewhat rotted greenery. Haul this lot out. Then clear the garden of dead annuals, rake leaves off paths and lawn areas and root out any weeds that have established themselves in beds. All this is destined for the compost bin. Remake the compost bin, adding fresh manure to it if possible.

Burn or bag and throw away any diseased plants, and all peach leaves when they drop. In a mixed garden that aims to be a haven for wildlife, leave some seed-heads on plants for birds in winter, and some leaves on the bed surface both to protect perennials and to serve as cover for overwintering creatures.

Spread any available well-rotted compost on the bed surfaces, to be gradually incorporated into the soil over winter. Spread manure on the beds if it is not in your compost.

A final, almost ritual, job is to clean up your tools. Reel in the hose and put it somewhere out of sight. In areas where the vine weevil is active, throw out all old soil from pots. Give the pots themselves a quick brush out and store somewhere upside down. Clean off the spade, fork and trowel and, if possible, put somewhere under cover. Turn the broom upside down so that it doesn't sit on its bristles. Oil and check your secateurs. If they are irreparably damaged, they are a great Christmas present for yourself. Go round the garden and pull up the bamboo canes that are no longer supporting plants and store them somewhere dry. If winters are hard, turn off water to outside taps and drain them.

All this may seem like an unnecessary chore, but in spring you will really appreciate it. Your pots will be dry and clean, ready to take the new compost and seeds. When you pick up your spade, your first job won't be to bang off caked mud. Your bamboo canes won't be rotted at the base, and your secateurs won't be stiff and rusty.

Winter

Winter is the best time to plant bare-root fruit trees and soft fruit, and to prune vines, apple and pear trees. It is also a time when container plants tend to be neglected and can actually suffer from drought. They need regular checking.

In places where the winter is wet, or very cold, put tender herbs that are in pots – lemon grass, tarragon, even thyme – somewhere out of the damp and protected from the cold.

If the winter threatens to be harsh, protect fig shoots by surrounding branches with straw, secured in place with sacking, or use plastic bubblewrap. Protect container-grown bay trees in the same way, and move them into a sheltered spot in the garden if possible.

Planting bare-rooted fruit trees Bare-rooted fruit trees are despatched from a nursery immediately they are lifted from the ground. The sooner they are back in the soil, the better. Dig a hole for the tree big enough for the roots to be spread out and not be bent. Dig some compost and bonemeal into the base of the hole and mix some in with the soil taken out of the bed. While you are digging the hole for the tree, it is a good idea to soak the roots in a bucket.

Place the tree into the hole with the graft union about 5cm (2in) above the level of the bed. When you're putting the soil back, try to avoid throwing large lumps in. Every now and then, shake the tree to settle the soil into and around the roots. Once all the roots are covered, firm in very well and water well. Stake with a short stake that supports the trunk to no more than half way so that the tree flexes a bit in the wind and so becomes strong enough to support itself. Place the stake on the far side of your main view so that most of the time it is obscured by the tree's trunk.

Forward planning Winter is a good time to think about the year to come. Order or buy seeds, remembering that most of us over-order and that, in the spring, unsown seeds in unopened new packets will cry out to be used.

General mainentance If there is a pleasant day, do any maintenance jobs to the boundaries like repairing trellis, putting up straining wire, painting fences etc. This is because the plants on the boundaries will be dormant, so much easier to work around. When doing this, however, try to step on the soil as little as possible, especially in areas where the soil is heavy. The more open these soils are through the winter, the more the frost breaks them down. So if you are going to spend time standing in a bed doing these jobs, put down boards to spread the load. Finish the job by lightly pointing compacted areas with a fork.

7

Starters · Main courses · Accompaniments · Desserts

recipes

The first cherries of summer, the first handful of French beans or new potatoes from the garden are so exciting that they are usually eaten as plainly as possible, the better to relish their freshness.

After a while, however, that excitement wanes, and it is then that some interesting recipes are needed if you are to continue to enjoy your garden's produce to the full. Since most Urban Edens are fairly small, and often contain a range of plants that are picked regularly, small quantities of fresh ingredients tend to be available at any one time, ideal for starters and appetisers. Urban Edens also usually feature quite a number of herbs, making it possible to prepare some wonderful dishes that cannot be made successfully with dried leaves.

Occasionally any crop will exceed all expectations. With even a few sprouting broccoli plants, a family, friends and neighbours will have enough to satisfy everyone's appetite for fresh steamed broccoli with butter. So a couple of the following recipes use comparatively large quantities of produce to help you enjoy even a glut crop when it's fresh.

Starters If you make one of these dishes, it is a 'starter'. If there is enough produce in your Urban Eden to make several, you can create an entire meal out of them. Tabbouleh, a salad of broad beans in their pods, some green salad (from your salad pot), some cheese or salami, and good bread – very heaven.

Tabbouleh – salad of cracked wheat

This astonishingly easy dish is deliciously refreshing. It is traditionally eaten by being scooped up in slightly chilled lettuce leaves. The weights given below are for guidance only: the exact proportions and quantities of parsley, onion, or mint depend largely on taste and on what is available. Take whole big leaves off the parsley and chop the stalks finely into this dish. *Serves 4*

250g (8oz) bulgur (cracked) wheat
500g (1lb) ripe tomatoes
Large bunch of parsley, including stalks
Large bunch of mint
    (about half as much as the parsley)
5 spring onions
1 lemon
6 tablespoons olive oil
Salt and ground pepper

Put the bulgur wheat in water for at least an hour, or overnight if you like it softer. Drain well.

Dice the tomatoes and chop all the herbs finely by hand. Slice the onions, and mix everything together lightly with a fork in a large bowl. Dress with oil and add lemon juice to taste, then add a pinch of salt and a sprinkling of pepper.

Raw mushroom salad with rosemary

An easy starter with a lovely taste that lingers in the mouth. It only works well with fresh rosemary as dried leaves are prickly, not soft. *Serves 6*

500g (1lb) fresh, closed mushrooms
Large sprig of rosemary
1 clove garlic, finely diced
4 tablespoons olive oil
1 tablespoon red wine vinegar
Salt

Slice the mushrooms quite thickly, a generous ½ cm (¼ in). Separate the rosemary needles from the sprig, and tear or cut them up coarsely. The more the needles are bruised, the stronger the taste of rosemary.

Place the garlic, olive oil and vinegar in a small bowl and whisk with a fork. If you are going to eat the dish immediately, pour all the vinaigrette over the mushrooms in a flat dish, turn them quickly so that all the slices get some liquid, sprinkle the rosemary over the dish, salt lightly and serve.

If you are making it ahead of the meal, pour half the vinaigrette over the mushrooms and turn them, then add the rosemary. Don't add salt, as this will draw all the water out of the mushrooms and make them mushy. The slices of mushroom will soak up vinaigrette like little sponges. Cover the dish with clingfilm and place in the fridge for an hour or so. Just before serving, allow it to return to room temperature (a touch chilled is quite pleasant in hot weather), add the rest of the vinaigrette, season and serve.

Steam the pods whole, then put them into a serving dish. Mix together the oil, vinegar and garlic to make a dressing and pour over the beans while still warm. Ideally, serve and eat just as the beans are cooling as they lose their colour and sharp taste when kept waiting.

Schezhuan runner beans

If you've got productive runner beans, you can quickly get overwhelmed by them. This recipe is an adaptation of one from Sophie Grigson's *Eat your Greens*.

Prepare all the ingredients first, ready to be tossed into the wok as needed. Dried shrimps are available from almost any oriental supermarket. They are superb in all sorts of things (fish stock, seafood risotto) and keep for a long time if stored in an airtight container. *Serves 4*

2 tablespoons dried shrimps
500g (1lb) runner beans
Sunflower oil
2 cloves garlic, thinly sliced
2cm (¾ in) fresh ginger, peeled and cut into matchsticks
½ teaspoon coarsely crushed Sichuan pepper or black
    peppercorns
½ teaspoon salt
1 tablespoon dark soy sauce
2 teaspoons rice vinegar or white wine vinegar
1 tablespoon sesame oil

Begin by putting the shrimps into just over half a cup of boiling water. Leave for 20 minutes, then drain, reserving the liquid, and chop the shrimps.

Slice the beans diagonally into long strips. Then deep-fry them for 5 minutes until they are lightly browned, or fry in a wok in about 2.5cm (1in) of oil. As the wok will be used later, this doesn't create extra washing up. You will probably

Salad of broad beans in their pods

Most broad beans are allowed to get big and hard before they are picked. But at an earlier stage, when the beans have just formed, and before the pod hardens, whole pods are delicious and tender. The length and breadth of the pod will vary depending on the variety, but they are usually best when no longer than 8cm (3in). *Serves 4*

At least 20 small broad bean pods
8 tablespoons olive oil
4 tablespoons vinegar
2 cloves garlic, finely chopped

have to deep-fry the beans in batches. It does take a little time, but is worth it. Drain the beans on kitchen paper.

If the wok was used, clear the oil, add a tablespoon of new sunflower oil and heat till it smokes. Add the garlic, ginger and pepper and stir-fry for a few seconds. Now add the chopped shrimps and stir-fry for a further 30 seconds. Stir in the salt, soy sauce and 5 tablespoons of shrimp water.

Finally, add the beans. Toss them in the sauce to coat, cover and – keeping the heat high – cook until virtually all the liquid has been absorbed. Check after a minute. The sauce should be caramelised and the beans a mahogany colour. If not, toss and cook for a further 30 seconds.

Remove from the heat, place in a bowl and mix with the vinegar and sesame oil. Allow the beans to cool. Serve cold.

Marinated kipper fillet salad

An irriesistible, outlandish dish! Rather than being sweet and vinegary like roll-mop herrings, this dish tastes smoky, with a blast of bay leaf. You can only make it if you have plenty of fresh bay leaves; dried bay leaves just don't have the same effect. For best results, assemble the dish a day or two before you need it to allow it to marinate thoroughly. *Serves 4*

2 kipper fillets
2 small onions
About 15 large fresh bay leaves
20 black peppercorns
Juice of 1 lemon

Remove the skin from the bottom of the kipper fillets. This is quite straightforward. Each kipper consists of two individual fillets; simply slip a sharp knife between the flesh of one of the fillets and the skin, and slide the knife along the skin. The fillet should come away in one piece.

Cut the skinned fillets into strips approximately as wide as a finger, slicing diagonally. Slice the onions into rings. Put layers of onion, kipper and bay leaves into a screwtop jar or bowl, adding black peppercorns and lemon juice as you go. When you have used up all the ingredients, seal the jar or cover the bowl with clingfilm, and place in the fridge.

After about a day, there will be extra liquid in the bottom of the container (a mix of onion juice, lemon juice and fish). Spoon this over the fish to continue the process of marinating. Eat within three days of assembling, serving with lettuce and generous quantities of well-buttered toast.

Broccoli and anchovy on pasta

Anchovies, chillies, garlic and sprouting broccoli sounds like a strange combination but it really works. Adjust the quantities to suit your taste. *Serves 2*

250g (8oz) sprouting broccoli spears
1 tablespoon olive oil
1 clove garlic
1 small dried chilli
2 whole salted anchovies
250g (8oz) pasta

Blanch the broccoli in very lightly salted boiling water (the addition of salted anchovies means this dish can become incredibly salty unless care is taken), drain immediately and put to one side. Wash the salt from the anchovies and peel the fillets away from the backbone. Or use anchovy fillets in olive oil, but pat all the oil off with a kitchen towel.

Roughly chop the garlic and heat it gently in the oil in a large sauté pan. When soft, add the anchovy fillets to the pan. Next add the chilli, deseeded and finely chopped.

When the anchovies have dissolved into the oil, add the blanched broccoli. Add a little hot water, cover and cook for about 10 minutes.

During this time, the pasta can be cooking. When everything is ready, pound the broccoli spears with the back of a wooden spoon so that a rough sauce is produced. Add a bit of water from the pasta if the sauce is not liquid enough.

When the pasta is done, drain well and put in a serving dish. Add the sauce, mix thoroughly and seve at once.

Oshitashi – salad of wilted garlic chives

An unusual starter that tastes of the sea. This is not a totally traditional Japanese version, but is our adaptation of it, one of the most delicious ways of using garlic chives.

If you do not have any nam pla, bonito or dried shrimp we urge you to start exploring your local oriental supermarket. These ingredients last for ages, and are delicious in all sorts of things *Serves 4*

2 large handfuls of garlic chive leaves
Some light fish stock or nam pla
  (Thai fish sauce)
Light soy sauce
Dried bonito or shrimp

Boil the garlic chives for one or two minutes, then plunge them into cold water. Drain and squeeze them dry between your hands, then place in a bowl.

Dress lightly with a mix of fish stock and soy. Top with grated bonito, or a sprinkling of chopped dried shrimp which, though unorthodox, makes a pleasing alternative.

Main courses

The one thing even a tiny Urban Eden and a gardener with not much time can easily produce, is large quantities of fresh herbs. Used boldy with meat, fish and eggs, they can transform what might otherwise be an ordinary meal.

Skewered tuna with sage

Sage is a beautiful plant, but underused except in stuffings. This recipe alone makes it worth growing. *Serves 4*

4 slices of tuna each the thickness of a finger
    weighing about 250g (8oz) per person
4 slices of bread the same thickness
Between 30 and 50 large fresh sage leaves
Olive oil
Salt and pepper
2 lemons

Cut the slices of tuna into squares not more than 2.5 x 2.5cm (1 x 1in). Remove the crusts and cut the bread into an equal number of the same size squares. Wash the sage leaves well.

Starting with bread, thread alternating squares of bread and tuna onto the skewers with a leaf of sage on either side of each piece of tuna.

Brush each skewer well with olive oil this takes more than you expect. Season with salt and pepper.

Grill the skewered tuna at a moderate temperature for at least 5 minutes a side (20 minutes in all is minimum, 30 is better). The aim is to cook the fish all the way through, with the outside of the bread nicely toasted. If the grill is too hot the outside will burn, and the inside remain raw.

Brush the tuna with olive oil as it grills if the skewers look at all dry. When cooked, squeeze lemon juice over the tuna and toast and serve with lemon quarters.

Sorrel omelette

The tang of sorrel perfectly complements the taste of buttery eggs in this superb omelette. *Serves 2*

Good handful of sorrel
30g (1oz) butter
Salt
3 or 4 eggs at room temperature

Wash and chop the sorrel and shake it dry. Melt all but a knob of the butter in a heavy-based saucepan and add the sorrel. Add a pinch of salt. Sorrel reduces in volume even more than spinach and within a few minutes it will be a grey-green purée ready to add to the omelette.

While the sorrel cooks, crack the eggs into a bowl. Stir with a fork sufficiently to mix the whites and yolks.

Heat the knob of butter in a big frying pan over a high heat until the butter stops fizzing (just before it starts to brown and smoke), then tip the egg mix into the pan and quickly lift some off the bottom with a spatula so that more raw egg contacts the pan. Do this several times and within 45 seconds – a minute at most – the omelette will be done. Spread the cooked sorrel over one half, slide the finished omelette out of the pan and fold it as it goes onto a warmed plate.

Chicken with tarragon

Tarragon goes beautifully with chicken, and there are countless recipes for it, with all sorts of embellishments. This is one of the simplest and most traditional. *Serves 4*

For a 1.5kg (3lb) fresh free-range chicken
    you need:
1 tablespoon tarragon leaves, roughly chopped
30g (1oz) butter
½ garlic clove, finely diced
Salt and pepper
Olive oil
Small glass of brandy

Preheat oven to 180°C/350°F/gas mark 4. Mix the tarragon with the butter, the garlic clove and salt and pepper to make a large green nugget. Pop this inside the chicken and brush the outside of the bird with olive oil.

Put the chicken in the preheated oven on a tray in a roasting dish on its side with a leg uppermost for 30 minutes. Turn it onto the other side so that the other leg is uppermost for another 30 minutes.

When it is cooked, take it from the oven and turn the heat down low.

If in any doubt whether the chicken is done, insert a sharp knife between the thigh and body of the chicken and press. If the juices that emerge are clear, it is cooked. If they're still bloody, the chicken needs a few minutes more but don't overcook the chicken or it just gets dry.

Put a small glass of brandy into a soup ladle and heat it over the stove. When the brandy moves very freely in the ladle, tip it over the chicken and light it. Tip the roasting dish from side to side until all the alcohol in the brandy has burnt off. Return the chicken and sauce to the cooling oven for 5 minutes, then serve with mashed potatoes to mop up the delicious sauce.

Pigeon breasts with tangy orange salsa

With a slight Oriental twist to cooking the pigeon and a Mexican touch to the salsa, this makes a light supper dish and is good served with crisply fried rosemary/garlic potatoes and a tasty green salad. *Serves 3–4*

8 plump pigeon breasts, each 100g
    (4oz) in weight
freshly ground black pepper
1 tablespoon light soy sauce
1 clove garlic, crushed
3 oranges
1 small red onion, finely chopped
1 fresh red chilli, deseeded and
    finely sliced
3–4 tablespoons fresh coriander,
    minced
3 tablespoons fresh mint, minced
Salt
Juice of ½ lime

Preheat the oven to 220°C/425°F/gas mark 7.

Make slashes in the skins of the pigeon, season with pepper and sprinkle over the soy sauce. Push slivers of garlic into the slashes. Cook on a rack in the oven for about 10–15 minutes until the skin is crispy.

Cut each orange into slices and these into small chunks. Mix these with the onion, the chilli and the herbs and season with a touch of salt and pepper. Pour in sufficient lime juice to leave a tangy salsa.

Serve with the pigeon breasts.

Accompaniments

Food grown with love, cooked as soon as it is picked, and brought immediately to table is such a rarity for most of us, that even if it is just a side dish, it is a luxury and should be served with a flourish.

Pesto

Pesto is wonderful on pasta, and is easy to make with a food processor. It is hard work and a struggle without one – making it in a normal-sized pestle and mortar means bits of basil leaf everywhere and lumpy pesto.

60g (2oz) fresh basil leaves
1 large clove garlic, crushed
1 tablespoon pine kernels
6 tablespoons extra virgin olive oil
Salt
30g (1oz) Parmesan cheese, freshly grated

Wash the basil leaves well and dry them in a salad spinner or by patting with a tea towel. Put the basil, garlic, pine kernels, olive oil and salt in the blender and blend until they have become a smooth purée.

Transfer to a bowl and stir in the cheese.

Pesto freezes well, but then you should omit the garlic from this recipe as the sulphur in the raw garlic turns the pesto bitter in the freezer. Fill ice-cube trays with garlic-less pesto. When it is frozen, knock out the lumps and store them in the freezer in a plastic bag. In winter, when you feel in need of a quick burst of summer, defrost a couple of pesto cubes, add some crushed garlic and eat with pasta or a rice salad. The plastic of the ice-cube tray may be dyed green, but this is a small price to pay!

Ahivetch

There are as many recipes for this in the Mediterranean as there are Irish recipes for Colcannon. It can be made with most vegetables, depending on what's growing well this week. This dish makes a good accompaniment to roast meat or flavourful dishes where something soothing is required.

3 tablespoons olive oil
1–2 red onions
4 garlic cloves, finely chopped
160g (6oz) French beans, topped and tailed
100g (4oz) fresh green peas
3 stalks celery, chopped
1 aubergine, sliced into rounds,
    salted and drained
2 courgettes, sliced into rounds,
    salted and drained
4 beef tomatoes, skinned and coarsely
    chopped
1 tablespoon tarragon or oregano
1 tablespoon thyme leaves
Salt and freshly ground black pepper
1 tablespoon flat-leafed parsley

In a heavy-bottomed frying pan, heat the oil and toss in the onion and garlic. Fry over gentle heat until the onion starts to colour. Stir in the vegetables except the tomatoes, and make sure they are all coated in oil. Stew gently for 10–15 minutes. Then add the tomatoes and herbs, cook over high heat for 5 minutes and season to taste. Arrange in a dish and sprinkle with parsley.

Roast potatoes with garlic and rosemary

It is hard to quantify how many potatoes are required to serve a given number, as people seem to eat roast potatoes until they have consumed them all. We have therefore erred on the side of generosity. *Serves 4*

2 tablespoons olive oil
1 kg (2lb) new potatoes
Salt and pepper
4 cloves garlic
Large sprig of rosemary

Preheat the oven to 200°C/400°F/gas mark 6. The cooking process can be speeded up if the roasting tin is put in the oven as it starts to heat with the olive oil in it.

Cut the scrubbed potatoes into small cubes about the thickness of a thumb. As soon as the oven is hot, toss the potatoes in the hot oil, season well with salt and pepper and return to the oven.

Dice the garlic and strip the leaves from the sprig of rosemary.

After 20 minutes toss the potatoes in the hot oil. Then after another 20 minutes, add the rosemary and garlic. Cook for a further 5 minutes, then serve immediately.

Braised lettuce with tomatoes

A spectacular way to use lettuces when they get a bit straggly or start to bolt. This recipe makes a tasty, crunchy vegetable dish, wonderful with lamb, or as a starter. *Serves 4*

4 small lettuces, whole
3 or 4 tomatoes or a half a tin of tomatoes
1 small onion
1 slice of ham or bacon
Olive oil
30g (1oz) butter
Salt and pepper
1 teaspoon sugar
Nutmeg
Parsley
12 stoned black olives (optional)

Wash the lettuces carefully, as you use them whole rather than stripping the leaves from the stems.

Blanch the whole lettuces by immersing them in a large pan of boiling water and letting the water come back to the boil before pulling them out of the water and draining them. You will probably have to blanch each in turn.

If using fresh tomatoes, skin them by putting them in a bowl and pouring some of the boiling water over them. After a moment in the water, the skins will just slip off. Chop roughly.

Dice the onion, ham or bacon and parsley and sweat it over a medium heat in a mixture of oil and butter in a sauté pan. When the onion has turned transparent, add the tinned tomatoes or chopped, skinned tomatoes.

Heat the mixture through and stir for a minute or two, then add the (now very limp) lettuces. Season well with salt, pepper, sugar and grated nutmeg. Cover and cook gently for 30 minutes.

If you like black olives, add them at this stage, and cook for another 10 minutes, then sprinkle with parsley to serve.

Desserts   We have got so used to the uniform and often somewhat bland taste of the fruit you can buy in the supermarket that the taste, texture and smell of desserts cooked with home-grown fruit can come as something of a revelation.

Tarte tatin

There are all sorts of ways of making this staple of French cuisine. Some are made with whole apples, others with sliced apples, and the pastry base varies hugely. This is a traditional version with a shortcrust pastry base. It is a little time-consuming to make, but worth it. It is best made with strongly flavoured, home-grown dessert apples. *Serves 6*

125g (4oz) flour
60g (2oz) butter
Salt
1 teaspoon cinnamon
125g (4oz) dark brown sugar
1kg (2lb) apples – any type,
    but no more than half of them cooking apples

Preheat the oven to 180°C/350°F/gas mark 4. To make the shortcrust pastry, put the flour into a fairly large bowl. Take butter from the fridge and while it is cold, add to the flour in small chunks. Add a pinch of salt. Working quickly with your thumb and fingertips, rub the butter with the flour gently till it resembles fine breadcrumbs. Don't squeeze it.

    Add just enough water so that you are able to form the breadcrumb-sized pieces of pastry into a ball. Less water is better than too much. Put this to one side in a cool place.

    Brush the bottom of a 20cm (8in) cake tin with butter and cover it with a circle of buttered greaseproof paper. Sprinkle cinnamon on the bottom followed by the sugar.

    Peel, core and thinly slice the apples by hand. Don't slice the apples in a food processor as they end up too thin.

Cherry clafoutis

A clafoutis is a sea of batter dotted with islands of fruit. It looks like something made professionally and yet it is very easy to make. *Serves 4*

500g (1 lb) Morello cherries
Sugar to taste
4 eggs
75g (3oz) plain flour
75g (3oz) caster sugar
500ml (16fl oz) single cream
Salt
Brandy

Preheat the oven to 200°C/400°F/gas mark 6. Stone the cherries and simmer them in a little sugar and water for about 5 minutes, then let them cool. To get a good contrast with the sweet batter of the clafoutis, the cherries should be slightly tart.

Make a loose batter by mixing the eggs, flour, sugar and cream and a pinch of salt in a large bowl until well combined. Butter an ovenproof container, ideally a 25cm (10in) tart tin, but clafoutis can successfully be made in any medium-sized shallow dish. The batter should be only about 2cm (¾ in) deep when poured, but the dish must be deep enough to contain it when it rises.

Pour the cherries into the dish, add brandy to taste, cover with batter, and bake in the preheated oven for about 30 minutes. The clafoutis is ready when the top is golden and firm to the touch.

Arrange the first layer carefully on the sugar and cinnamon in the tin. It should be done with care because this will be the top of the tart. Continue adding slices, pressing them down till all the apples are used up. This can be done quite quickly and roughly.

Roll the pastry out to less than 1cm (¼ in) thickness, so that it is roughly the size of the tin, then place it on top of the apples and press it down gently.

Bake in the preheated oven for between 30 and 40 minutes until the pastry is golden. Allow to cool in the tin, then turn it upside down and remove the tin and greaseproof paper.

Tarte tatin is best served chilled, with some chilled fromage frais, crème fraîche or double cream.

Mixed fruit crumble

The humble mixed fruit crumble is one of the most enchanting of puddings, equally delicious warm from the oven, or gooey and cold from the fridge the day after it was made. It is a superb way of using apples, pears, plums, damsons, gooseberries and greengages. The addition of even a very few tasty, ripe blackberries, blackcurrants or blueberries to a plain apple or pear crumble perks it up a lot. *Serves 6*

250g (8oz) plain flour
125g (4oz) sugar
125g (4oz) butter
750g–1kg (1½–2lb) fruit
   of your choice
Extra sugar to taste

Preheat the oven to 200°C/400°F/gas mark 6. There is an easy way to calculate crumble topping: mix two parts flour with one part butter. For the adventurous and unconventional, oat flakes can be used instead of all the flour (for a crunchier topping) and various brown sugars can be substituted for plain white if darker flavours are preferred. Enough crumble mix is needed to cover the fruit completely to a depth of about 2cm (¾ in).

To make the crumble, mix the flour and sugar in a bowl and cut the butter into it. Using fingertips and quick pinching movements, create breadcrumb-sized pieces of butter and flour and sugar. Do not squeeze the mixture; you need a very open mix of rough crumbs of butter covered with flour and sugar.

Cut the fruit into bite-sized chunks and arrange in an ovenproof dish. Sprinkle extra sugar over sharp fruit such as damsons or gooseberries. Gently spoon the uncooked crumble mix over the fruit so that it is completely covered.

Bake in the preheated oven for between 35 and 40 minutes. The crumble is done when the top is golden.

Quince preserve

This is delicious at the end of a meal, savoured with coffee and a dish of mixed nuts and other dried fruits.

Quinces
Sugar

Wash the quinces, and quarter them to remove the cores, but do not peel them. Cut into chunks and steam them until soft. Weigh the cooked quince and put aside the same amount of sugar. Purée the quince in a blender and add the sugar.

Then cook the sweetened pulp in a saucepan until it is a deep orange and starts to come away from the sides when you stir it.

Line a baking tray with greaseproof paper and pour the pulp into the tray so that it is between 1–5cm (¼–2in) deep. Put in a just-warm oven for several hours until the paste is dry. An oven that you have just been roasting a joint in is perfect.

Once the paste is dry, cut it into squares and store in an airtight container for up to two weeks.

suggested urban eden plants

The aim of these plant pages is to give a simple introduction to the easier and more decorative edible plants, which urban gardeners may not previously have thought of growing. Each description details the conditions the plants prefer, along with real-life tips and hints to make growing easier. Where there are lots of varieties to choose from, the ones we suggest tend to be those that are relatively resistant to disease, that crop relatively freely and taste superb.

The list is by no means exhaustive, but provides suggestions so that an Urban Eden gardener can begin many delightful (and occasionally frustrating) years of experimentation.

We haven't recommended plants such as cabbages, cauliflowers and hearting lettuces that require a significant amount of room in return for a single crop. They don't really give enough value to justify their inclusion in the average small urban plot. Nor do we advocate heavy-cropping commercial plants as they tend to produce crops little different from those available in supermarkets.

These plant pages divide edible plants into herbs, salads, vegetables and fruit. This is, of course, completely artificial and easy to quibble with. Sorrel is used as a salad and as a vegetable but here it is classified with salads since most people regard it as such nowadays. Rocket is also part herb, part salad, and is here found among the salads.

8

Herbs

If there is a particular herb that you use a lot, grow several specimens even if space is limited. If you only have one, it is not uncommon for it to die – or at least fail to thrive – due to overpicking. With two or more the cook can alternate between plants, which gives them a chance to get their strength back between assaults.

In summer, when herbs are growing strongly, it is a good idea to store some leaves. During a hot spell, dry some oregano and marjoram simply by clipping sprigs, and hanging them in the sun. Sun-dried fennel seeds are also delicious. Deep freeze the herb leaves that you will use in cooking during the winter: bay, basil, tarragon, parsley.

BASIL
Ocimum basilicum
Annual
Height 20–45cm (8–18in)
Best in pots
This sun-loving popular herb has dozens of uses in the kitchen, and is a staple of Mediterranean cookery. Most people find basil very easy to grow, though a few have problems. It is ideal for the kitchen windowsill or a sunny spot within easy reach. The easiest type to grow is Bush basil *Ocimum basilicum minimum*, an attractive plant with very small leaves and a compact bushy habit. It does not have such a strong taste as larger-leafed Sweet basil *O. basilicum* which is the best-flavoured variety with large leaves but a rather straggling habit. Purple-leafed basil *O. basilicum purpurascens* is less easy to grow and has a very floppy habit, and dark-leafed Sacred basil *O. tenuiflorum* is aromatic and excellent for Thai cooking but not for pesto. Though it is best to use basil leaves fresh, they can be frozen. Basil does not dry.

Cultivation: Sow basil seeds indoors sparingly in pots with good drainage on a sunny sill in late spring; only move outside when there is no risk of a frost. Transplant to a bigger pot when seedlings are large enough to handle, or into rich, well-drained soil. If you buy ready-grown plants, the basil sold early in the season will have been forced in a greenhouse and will have difficulty going into less well-regulated conditions; none the less these basil plants transplant well later in the season.

Pinch out flowers when they appear, in order to prolong the life of the plants for up to a month.

If plants go black at the base, pull them up immediately and throw them away.

Basil is a good companion for tomatoes as it is reputed to help keep the tomatoes relatively pest-free.

BAY
Laurus nobilis
Perennial
Height 30cm–8m (12in–25ft)
Good in containers and beds
A very easy, rewarding plant to grow, bay is evergreen, aromatic, and the leaves contribute an essential taste to many dishes. Although trees grown outdoors in ideal conditions can attain great heights, bay trees can also be kept small in a pot indoors or outside, or topiarised into elegant shapes in containers or beds.

Cultivation: Buy a nursery-grown bay or take a rooted offshoot from a friend's tree. Bays prefer full sun and fertile well-drained soil but will survive in semi-shade and in a container with fairly poor soil as long as they are not allowed to dry out, and protected from wind and frost.

Problems: Very susceptible to scale insect. Clean them off with a cloth and warm, soapy water. The leaves of container-grown plants in cities get covered in a black filmy coat.

Clean with warm soapy water. If you find new growth curling and going bright yellow, pick off affected leaves and burn them as you may have been visited by the Bay Sucker, a leaf-mining insect.

CHERVIL
Anthriscus cerefolium
Annual
Height 30–45cm (12–18in)
Grow outside in the ground
A shade-loving herb with a spicy, aniseed flavour, chervil looks like cow parsley and lends a planting a country garden look. The curly-leafed variety *A. crispum* has a milder flavour.

Cultivation: Seeds germinate rapidly. Sown in a moist shady spot in spring, the plants will be ready for cutting after only 6–8 weeks. In mild areas chervil can be grown through winter. Remove flowering stems to ensure a continual supply of leaves that can be cropped from when the plant is 10cm (4in) tall.

CHIVES
Allium schoenoprasum
Perennial
Height 30cm (12in)
Good for windowboxes, pots and beds
Easy to grow, beautiful in leaf and flower, and delicious. The attractive purple flowers can be left on the plants all summer.

Cultivation: Chives grow well either from seeds planted in spring or bought-in plants. They are quite tolerant of where they are planted, but prefer a good soil and plenty of sun. Once a clump becomes mature, split it to encourage further growth: dig the clump up in early spring and tease it into several mini-clumps, then replant.

Harvesting: Treat chives like grass: just snip leaves (and flowers) as required.

CORIANDER

Coriandrum sativum

Annual

Height to 60cm (2ft)

Good in containers inside or outside, and in beds

A powerful-flavoured herb that tastes wonderful fresh and is an essential ingredient for many dishes. Grow a pot on the window-sill, and snip leaves as required. The whole plant, including the seeds and root, can be used in cooking.

Cultivation: In spring sow seeds directly into the pot or into light, well-drained soil in early summer, as coriander dislikes being moved. If you buy a small plant pot into a bigger container or the ground without disturbing the roots. Place it in a sunny position, and if you grow it indoors make sure air can flow around it as it dislikes too much damp and humidity. It runs to seed very quickly so keep picking leaves from the top to prevent early flowering.

Coriander seems to prefer to have its roots shaded from direct sun; a top dressing of stones around the plant can help.

DILL

Anethum graveolens

Annual

Height to 1m (3ft)

Dill looks very similar to fennel, with luxurious feathery foliage and tiny yellow flowers in flattened umbels. Both leaves and seeds are very useful.

Cultivation: Start seeds in early spring indoors or outside under cover in pots or plugs. Don't use seed trays as dill dislikes being moved. Germination is slow – 2 to 4 weeks depending on warmth and atmosphere – but when the seedlings are large enough to handle and all danger of frost is past, plant into well-drained soil in full sun.

Alternatively, simply buy a plant from a retailer. Don't plant dill in freshly manured soil. Keep plants well watered to prevent them running to seed in hot weather.

Harvesting: Pick leaves any time once plant has reached maturity. Cut stalks off flower heads once seeds begin to ripen and dry them in a paper bag.

Problems: Don't compost dill seeds as they remain viable for up to 3 years.

FENNEL

Foeniculum vulgare

Perennial

Height to 1.5m (5ft)

Best in beds, but very decorative in a large container

A superb plant for the Urban Eden, fennel is easy to grow and good-looking. The leaves are useful in salads and stocks, the seeds delicious raw, or dried. Herb fennel is distinct from its relative the vegetable Florence fennel. Common green fennel has bright-green foliage and large umbels of yellow flowers in summer, while bronze fennel has attractive bronze feathery foliage.

Both are so attractive that they are worth growing for their ornamental value alone.

Cultivation: Most Urban Edens are only big enough to take one or at most two fennels, so rather than sow seed just buy a small nursery-grown fennel and plant it in fertile, well-drained soil in a sunny position. Don't allow fennel to become waterlogged or it can suffer root rot.

Although perennial, the plant begins to flag after a couple of years. To renew, either select a good self-seeded youngster (it self-seeds readily) or dig up the parent plant and split off a healthy small shoot to plant in a new location.

Harvesting: Pick leaves any time for use in stocks and soups or for fish dishes. The fresh seeds add a wonderful, aniseed flavour to salads, pasta sauces, risotto and fish. Dried, the seed develops a lovely smoky, aniseed flavour.

GARLIC

Allium sativum

Perennial usually grown as annual

Height 30cm (12in)

Interesting in containers, most productive in beds

Cultivation: Separate a garlic bulb into individual cloves and plant about 2cm (1in) deep in full sun in rich soil in late autumn, with cloves about 20cm (8in) apart to get large bulbs, but you can still get a harvest of small bulbs if you plant closer together. Keep well watered, and harvest in mid to late summer when the leaves begin to die down. You can plant in spring for late summer harvest, but autumn-planted cloves make bigger bulbs.

Plant garlic under peaches and it may help prevent peach leaf curl, or near roses to alleviate black spot.

Problems: White rot which causes yellowing of the foliage and a white fungal growth on the bulbs. Remove infected plants and don't plant garlic again in the same area of the garden.

LEMON GRASS

Cymbopogon citratus

Tender perennial

Height to 45cm (18in)

Grow in containers in cool areas

A tender aromatic tropical grass. In cooler climates overwinter lemon grass in a conservatory or greenhouse if possible. Keep dry over winter.

Cultivation: Lemon grass grows well in a generous container at least 25cm (10in) deep full of well-drained compost in a sunny position, and makes a handsome show on a large windowsill.

Harvesting: With a small plant, simply chop off a few leaves and add to dishes. With a bigger clump, break off a whole stalk. The taste in the central core of the stalk is the best.

Problems: Very tender and susceptible to overwatering, particularly in cool weather.

MARJORAM/OREGANO
Origanum spp
Perennial or treat as annual
Height from mound-forming to 45cm (18in)
Very good in containers, windowboxes and beds
Marjoram, or oregano, is a very useful and adaptable herb. The widely grown rather sprawling pot marjoram *Origanum onites* has pale-green leaves and pink or purple flowers in summer. Greek oregano *O. vulgare ssp hirtum* is deliciously flavoured, with aromatic grey-green hairy leaves, and clusters of tiny white flowers. Golden marjoram *O. vulgare* 'Aureum' forms a neat mound and has very attractive fine-flavoured golden leaves which are slightly hairy.

Sweet marjoram *O. vulgare* is strong-flavoured and slightly tender, so grown as an annual in cool climates.

Cultivation: Oregano can be grown from seed in spring, but requires bottom heat and germination can be erratic. Unless many plants are required in the garden, it is just as economical to buy a couple of good plants and pot them out in a sunny position with well-drained soil. The golden varieties prefer to be shaded from the very hot sun. Even the hardiest marjorams dislike very wet winters, and containers must have very good drainage.

Harvesting: The taste improves with drying, especially if it is dried in the sun.

MINT
Mentha spp
Perennial
Height to 60cm (2ft)
Best when contained
There are many mints, all of which are hardy. Most are invasive and if planted in a border can easily become a problem. Mint is best planted in a container sunk in a bed; lift the container every year or two, separate out the roots, refill with fresh compost and replace. Apple mint *Mentha suaveolens* has apple scent and flavour; it is very good to plant alongside paths for the fragrance, and attractive with bright-green leaves and pinkish-white flowers. Moroccan mint *M. spicata* 'Moroccan' has a strong, clear taste and is excellent in cooking and for mint tea. Common mint or garden mint *Mentha spicata* has green pointed leaves with serrated edges and purple/mauve flowers; it is generally considered to be the best for cooking and makes a great mint jelly.

Cultivation: Grow from a plant, not seed. Mints will tolerate virtually any aspect and soil but flourish best in moist shady places. Different varieties planted beside each other lose their individual flavours.

MYRTLE
Myrtus communis
Perennial
Height 60cm – 1.5m (2–5ft)
Content in large container
Myrtle boasts attractive reddish bark which becomes grey and cracked with age, pale-green oval leaves, scented creamy-white flowers in summer followed by purplish-black berries. Ornamental, evergreen and scented, it imparts a delicious flavour to roast meat.

Cultivation: Not entirely hardy in cooler climates, myrtle needs a sunny sheltered position, and fertile, well-drained soil. Trim in spring to maintain shape.

PARSLEY
Petroselinum crispum
Treat as annual
Height and spread 45–60cm (18–24in)
Excellent in containers and beds
Parsley is one of the most essential culinary herbs. Its subtle yet strong fresh iron taste adds an extra dimension to all sorts of dishes. Curly parsley has bright-green, crinkly leaves and is best for garnish and display, while French or flat-leafed parsley has flat, dark-green leaves and is the better of the two for cooking.

Cultivation: Parsley seeds take a long time to germinate – 4–6 weeks – and young plants hate root disturbance. So it is worth considering simply buying a couple of plants rather than sowing seed. When the plants have filled the original pots, transfer each to a significantly bigger pot or into the ground by knocking them out and filling in around the root ball in the new pot with good, strong new soil. Water well and the plants will grow excellently. Parsley is a hungry plant and needs well-manured soil when planted into the garden.

ROSEMARY
Rosmarinus officinalis
Perennial
Height to 1m (3ft)
Grow in containers or beds
A useful aromatic evergreen shrub with needle-shaped leaves and blue (or less often pink or white) flowers. You can choose upright forms such as the very fragrant Sissinghurst blue or the pale-blue-flowered Miss Jessop's upright which makes a lovely, neat hedge. Severn sea is an attractive low-

growing form, excellent as a ground-cover plant, with bright mid-blue flowers. There are also white and pink varieties, all with much the same flavour.

Cultivation: Buy nursery-grown plants and place in well-drained soil in a sheltered, sunny position. Bushes get tired within 5–6 years, so consider replacing them then.

Rosemary is said to repel carrot fly from carrots and to be beneficial when grown close to sage.

Problems: Cuckoo spit aphid loves rosemary. Rub the protective white foam off with your fingers, revealing the fat, pale-green aphids beneath, then squash them.

SAGE
Salvia officinalis
Perennial
Height and spread to 60cm (2ft)
Grow in containers or beds
This aromatic and ornamental evergreen shrub flowers in late summer with either violet-purple or pink blossoms above downy leaves of various colours.

Common garden sage *Salvia officinalis* has thin oval leaves and is best for the cook. *S. officinalis icterina* has attractive green and gold variegated leaves, and *S. officinalis purpurescens* has purple leaves and mauve-blue flowers which make the whole plant look very striking.

Cultivation: Sage likes well-drained, acid-free soil in a warm, dry site. Prune in spring and after flowering to keep plants bushy. Sage bushes age rapidly, and need replacement every 3–5 years. They layer easily, so this is a good way to keep the stock going.

Sage is said to be a good companion for grape vines.

TARRAGON
Artemisia dracunculus
Perennial
Height to 60cm (2ft)
Best in containers in cooler climates
French tarragon has a delicate flavour and numerous uses in the kitchen. It has smooth, green, long, narrow leaves held on long stems, and tiny yellow flowerheads that rarely produce seed except in hot climates. Do not plant Russian tarragon *Artemisia dracunculus dracunculoides as it* has practically no taste, is coarse and invasive.

Cultivation: French tarragon is rather tender and somewhat temperamental, only flourishing in dry conditions and hot sun. Grow from nursery-grown stock, planting on into a larger pot or well-drained soil in a very sheltered and sunny position. Do not overwater. It will need protection to get through a cold winter, but even if you lose it each winter, it is still worth growing.

If plants overwinter, they will still need renewing every 2–3 years. In the spring, knock the old plant out of the pot. You are likely to find that the original plant is worn out, but that two or three younger ones have spread from the roots. Separate these out and repot into a fairly large container, allowing room for the roots to spread and new plants to be established. They will grow for a year more.

After that, it may be necessary to buy in a new plant especially as young tarragon tastes stronger than tarragon from an older plant.

Harvesting: There are two ways of picking tarragon, depending on how often it is used and how much is available. The obvious way is to clip a branch, and then strip off the leaves. However, if the plant is growing slowly, and there is not enough spare foilage to provide a whole sprig, go up and down the branches pulling the longest leaves off the stem individually.

THYME
Thymus spp
Perennial
Height to 30cm (12in)
Flourishes in pots
Excellent for the Urban Eden, thyme is evergreen, has a delicate and attractive flower which bees love, the leaves are very aromatic and it can be used in many dishes. Common thyme *Thymus vulgaris* is the best for the kitchen and a delightful-looking little plant, that has woody stems, tiny dark-green oval leaves and lilac flowers that bees adore. *T. vulgaris* 'Silver Posie' has very pretty grey-silver variegated leaves and pale-pink flowers, while *T. vulgaris* 'Golden King' has leaves edged in yellow. *T. citriodorus* 'Silver Queen' has grey-silver variegated leaves, pink flowers and a very strong lemon scent, which makes it an excellent herb for chicken, fish and rice dishes.

Cultivation: Thymes suit container-growing, with extra gravel added in the compost for additional drainage, or grow in a sunny position in very well-drained soil. The plants hate being cold and wet in winter. In a rich soil, the plant will grow vigorously but will have hardly any taste. Thymes tend to die back in the centre after 3–4 years, so replace plants regularly. Trim after flowering to stop the centres from going woody.

Thyme will get discouraged if picked too hard, too regularly. It is best to plant several plants, or layer an existing plant as soon as possible to ensure continuous supply.

Salads

For much too long 'salad' had a bad press, the word conjuring up pictures of damp, limp, tasteless lettuce leaves or sugary, pale crisp ones. The revolution is here, in the sense that the wheel is turning, and turning back to the salads of old, which were, centuries ago, composed of myriad different leaves, with clearly defined tastes: hot, cool, sweet and bitter. Even a small Urban Eden can provide all that, with hot rocket, sweet basil, some bitter sorrel and some cool young lettuce.

If those are in the garden, and there are the salad-like herbs too (basil, chives, coriander, fennel and parsley) salads can become really exciting, varying between a hot rocket and parmesan salad with a sweet balsamic vinegar dressing; a herb salad of chives, coriander, sorrel and basil with some bought-in lettuce; or just lettuce and basil and boiled new potatoes, with a warm dressing of bacon and a sharp wine vinegar. Heaven.

As with herbs, this selection is no more than a starter pack, a few of the many that can be grown successfully even on a windowsill. All salads are as happy growing in tubs as in the ground, and their range of colours, shapes and sizes can make for very decorative container plantings.

CORN SALAD / LAMB'S LETTUCE / MACHE
Valerianella locusta
Height to 10cm (4in)
A subtle-tasting, pretty little salad plant with low-growing deep-green rosettes of leaves. Long popular in France, it has more of a texture in the mouth than a flavour. It can be grown as cut-and-come-again and will provide salad leaves in winter.

Cultivation: Sow seeds in fertile soil from mid to late spring for crops in summer. For crops in winter, sow mid to late summer. Corn salad prefers a sheltered position in partial shade. In full sun it tends to go to seed quickly.

Harvesting: Pick leaves as required, or take the whole plant when mature. Do not pick too many leaves off one plant at any one time as it will weaken.

WILD GARLIC / RANSOMES
Allium ursinum
Perennial
Height to 30cm (12in)
An underrated plant, wild garlic is ideal for ground cover in an Urban Eden. Plants produce clusters of scented white flowers in spring, and the young spring leaves are eaten, not the bulbs.

Cultivation: Sow seed in autumn in moist, fertile soil in semi-shade or full shade. Wild garlic with upright white flowers is not very invasive; wild garlic with floppy white flowers is much more so.

LETTUCE
Lactuca sativa
Height to 30cm (12in)
Hearting lettuces such as Cos and Webb varieties are not the best choice for most Urban Edens. They take up quite a lot of room, don't look like much until they are quite big, then all at once there is a whole lettuce that has to be consumed immediately. Where several have been planted at the same time, it becomes a race to eat them before they bolt.

The cut-and-come-again mixes that are now widely available are a different matter. They are easy to grow, quick to mature, look attractive and add a soft, sweet note to a salad. It is thrilling for a child to have a sandwich with one leaf of lettuce from their own salad pot (see page 38).

There are varieties to suit all tastes and seasons: our favourites are Black Seeded Simpson with lovely, very lobed pale-green leaves; Lollo Rosso with leaves tinged red with a wavy margin and the dark-red-leafed Red Salad Bowl. There are dozens more.

Cultivation: Lettuce seed does not germinate at high temperatures, so it is best sown outside or on a cool sill. In hot weather, sow seed at the end of the day. Sow summer crops from mid-spring to midsummer. Sow winter hardy varieties from late summer to early autumn. For a steady supply, sow every 6 weeks or so.

Scatter seed on the surface of well-tilled fertile soil and rake a litle over the top, then thin lettuces when they reach about 10cm (4in). Lettuces prefer cool conditions with lots of light and regular water; they bolt if they dry out.

Harvesting: Simply pull off the bigger leaves, or cut the hearts out of the bigger lettuces in the mix to encourage them to break again from the stump.

NASTURTIUM
Tropaeolum majus
Height to 30cm (12in) but spreads far and wide unless a bush variety
Easy to grow, good flowers, interesting-tasting leaf, edible seeds and habits that range from prostrate to climbing: what more could a plant do? Alaska is a bush variety with variegated leaves and red and yellow flowers. The Gleam series has a semi-trailing habit, double flowers in single colours or mixes which include scarlet, yellow or orange. The Jewel series is a bush variety with red, yellow and orange flowers. The Whirlybird series has flowers in a mixture or single colours. Empress of India has beautiful dark-red flowers and small dark leaves.

Cultivation: In theory, nasturtium seeds can be sown where they are to grow, but in practice, if there is a slug or snail in the vicinity, nasturtium seedlings are a favourite snack. So it is best to sow a few seeds in a pot, grow until plants have several leaves, then transplant into position. Pick seeds as they form to encourage continuous flowering. Nasturtiums can be grown up plants and pea sticks.

Harvesting: The young leaves and flowers

have a delicious, peppery flavour and are a pleasant addition to a mixed salad. The seeds are hot, and may be used in place of capers.

ROCKET
Eruca vesicaria
Biennial, treat as annual in cool climates
Height 10–30cm (4–12in)
This popular salad herb has a pungent, hot taste. It is very easy to grow, ready to eat very quickly, and tolerates regular cutting. It has rather a messy habit, and runs to flower easily with a small yellow-white flower that becomes white through the summer.

Cultivation: Sow outside from mid-spring onwards in batches, repeat sowing regularly as rocket runs to seed quite easily. Grow almost anywhere: the hotter the position, the stronger the taste, but the quicker it will flower and seed. You can sow in autumn for a winter crop as long as it does not freeze hard, and rocket will sometimes overwinter. Overwintered rocket has a stronger flavour than young rocket, so when using it in a salad, requires a sweeter vinegar.

Harvesting: The leaves are ready to pick within 6 weeks. Pick from then on to encourage new growth. Alternatively, cut the whole plant to a bud low on the stem for a vigorous new shoot. If the plant starts to flower, the leaves lose some of their flavour.

SORREL
Rumex
Perennial
Height 30–60cm (1–2ft)
The lance-shaped, bright-green leaves of sorrel taste sharp, somewhat lemony. Broad-leaved sorrel *Rumex acetosa* has large, fairly thick leaves and is good for sauces. Buckler leaf sorrel *Rumex scutatus* has delicate leaves which are best in salads. Sorrel is an excellent plant for a slightly shady windowbox.

Cultivation: Sow seeds in late spring outside, or buy a small nursery-grown plant. Sorrel tolerates sun or partial shade and, once established, is very hardy. It prefers well-drained, acidic, moisture-retentive soil. Every couple of years dig up the plant, divide, and replant the young plants.

Harvesting: Use as cut-and-come-again. Pick off flowers to keep the plants going. Sorrel leaves freeze well.

Vegetables
The vegetables listed here are all relatively easy to grow, don't take up much space or, if they are large, look interesting or taste extra delicious.

Vegetables tend to be a bit more of a challenge to grow than herbs, which is one of the reasons why they are so exciting to have in the garden. Waiting for the first broad beans to get big enough to eat and hoping that no marauding pest is going to get there first reminds the pampered city-dweller what it must be like to be a farmer. It also helps explain why so many of them resort to chemicals.

GLOBE ARTICHOKE
Cynara scolymus
Perennial
Height 1.2–1.5m (4–5ft)
Globe artichoke plants look like thistles on steroids. They are large and impressive plants, with blue-grey serrated leaves held on thick stems that reach upwards. The flower buds – which are the artichokes themselves – are impressively large, and if allowed to flower, open into a huge, purple thistle-like flower.

Cultivation: Grow from a nursery-grown plant. Artichokes like a sunny position, and well-drained fertile soil that doesn't dry out too much in summer, and suffer badly if there is waterlogging in winter. Once established, they are very tough, but the edible flower buds only reach a good size when grown in optimum conditions. Several of these flower buds may be produced in even the first year of growth, and an established plant produces a large number. Leave a few on the plant to flower as they are spectacular.

ASPARAGUS
Asparagus officinalis
Perennial
Height 1.2m (4ft)
Possible in very large containers, at least 45cm (18in) deep such as a bathtub
If you have space for a very deep, richly manured and fairly sunny bed, or part of a bed, asparagus is a marvellous plant. It has delicious delicate spears, and if some are left uncut they go on to become very tall, filmy, grey-green ferny foliage, much loved by flower arrangers. Each plant requires 45cm square (18in square).

Asparagus are very greedy but as long as they have enough manure will tolerate most soils. They also require good drainage. They favour deep beds of sheltered, well-drained soil which has had lots of organic matter added to it. If growing in a container, use a very strong mix of up to 50 percent manure, 50 percent soil-based compost, with grit added or drainage. Dress the plant with well-rotted manure every winter.

No-one but professionals plants asparagus seed. Instead, buy an established plant as a 'crown'. As soon as you get the crowns, soak for an hour, then plant in a hole 15cm (6in) deep on a low mound of earth with the roots spread out. All-male varieties are preferable, otherwise energy is wasted in the production of seeds, and seedlings will come up all over the garden.

Harvesting: Allow a newly planted crown two years' full growth to become established.

In year three, cut a proportion of the foliage spears in spring when they are about 10cm (4in) long. Cut below the surface of the soil. A contented asparagus plant should crop for the next 20 years!

AUBERGINES

Solanum melongena
Annual
Height 1m (3ft)
A subtropical plant that looks wonderful in fruit. Where the climate permits, they are excellent in containers, otherwise difficult to grow unless you have a greenhouse. Moneymaker crops well, with long, tasty fruit; Easter egg produces an egg-shaped white aubergine, and Little fingers produces attractive, small, narrow fruit.

Cultivation: Plant seeds indoors in spring, transplant into 30cm (12in) pots on a sunny windowsill after 6 weeks' growth when the plant is strong. Stake firmly, tying as they grow. Put out into the garden in early summer. Water sparingly but regularly. Feed with tomato fertiliser once the flower trusses form. Pinch out the growing tip when the plant is about 30cm (1ft) tall. Plants crop in late summer/early autumn. Allow 4 to 6 large fruits, or up to 15 small ones, remove the rest of the flowers and pinch out side shoots as they form.

Harvesting: Cut fruit from the vine with a sharp knife to minimise risk of infection in the wound when they are the right colour and about 7.5–15cm (3–6in) long, depending on variety.

FRENCH BEANS

Phaseolus vulgaris
Annual
Height from 10cm (4in) dwarf varieties to 120cm (4ft) climbers
Dwarf varieties are good in containers

French beans are particularly good for small gardens, as dwarf and bush varieties are attractive, prolific, and they produce delicious beans over a long period. Some varieties have highly ornamental purple pods. Climbers can adorn a wall or make a centrepiece in a bed trained on a tripod.

Cultivation: French beans need warmth to germinate and dislike cold and wet soils, so sow indoors for transplanting after frost has past, or outdoors when the soil has warmed. They like sheltered, sunny positions, and well-composted soil. Climbing French beans are particularly sensitive to wind, while dwarf varieties grow well in containers.

The roots of beans and other legumes fix nitrogen, so when the plant has finished cropping, cut the top from the roots and leave them in the soil to release their nitrogen.

BEETROOT

Beta vulgaris esculenta
Annual
Height 15cm (6in)
Miniature varieties are excellent for containers.
Pity the poor beetroot. It is so often grown till it is big and tough, then boiled and soused in malt vinegar. It deserves much better. Small fresh beetroots, roasted, are a gourmet treat, and the fresh pink tops make a pleasantly sweet addition to a salad. Boltardy is a globe-shaped beetroot that is bolt-resistant, suitable for early sowing, with good texture and flavour. Detroit is a baby, globe-shaped beet. Pronto and Monaco are mini beets which are sown thickly and harvested when about 2cm (1in) in diameter. *Albina Vereduna* 'Sunwhite' is a white globe-shaped beetroot.

Cultivation: Sow clusters of seeds from mid-spring to late autumn, in an open site, with fertile, light and well-drained soil, preferably manured for a previous crop. Keep beetroot well watered. If growing in containers, use

rich soil-based compost. Beetroot takes 2 or 3 months before it can be harvested. Don't let them get too big: golfball-sized have the best and sweetest taste.

Problems: Alkaline soil can cause yellow blotches on the leaves (manganese deficiency). Excess water will result in big leaves and small roots. If the plants dry out, the root will go woody. After a dry spell, watering will cause the root to split.

SPROUTING BROCCOLI

Brassica oleracea italica
Annual
Height to 90cm (3ft)
This is a superb winter crop for a small garden. It produces edible shoots through winter and into late spring, grows well on poor soils, and can tolerate cold. It prefers a sunny position.

Cultivation: Broccoli appreciates a rich soil, but too much manure will encourage more leaf than sprout. It will not grow satisfactorily on shallow or sandy soils, and should be protected from strong winter winds.

For autumn and winter crops, sow seed outdoors from mid to late spring. For late winter and early spring cropping, sow in late summer. Stake the plants in late autumn as broccoli can become top-heavy and keel over.

Harvesting: Cut the sprouts while the flowers are still in tight bud. Harvest regularly otherwise sprouting will stop. Do not cut every head off at any one cutting.

CARROTS

Daucus carota
Some varieties good in containers
For those who adore carrots, the good news is that by cunning use of different varieties, and by succession sowing, carrots should be available from the garden for much of the

year. Look for quick-growing early croppers such as Amsterdam and the longer and fatter-rooted Nantes, and long-storing Chantenay types with short, thick, tapering roots. Others such as the ever-popular Autumn King have good storing qualities. Catalogues offer white, pale-yellow, orange and even reddish-purple varieties in various shapes, many specifically bred to resist carrot fly. There are also miniature varieties and short-rooted types particularly good for containers.

Cultivation: Carrots prefer light soils which have been manured the autumn before sowing, and soil should always be loose, friable and warm for sowing seeds 2cm (1in) deep. A sheltered position is best. As they grow, and the carrots swell, pull a little soil up around the carrot to prevent the top of it going green, and to deter carrot fly. Growing in amongst a mixed planting of flowers or alliums seems to reduce carrot fly attack, as does growing them beside a fence more than 60cm (2ft) tall because carrot flies are low flyers. If a few plants are left to flower, carrots will attract many beneficial insects.

Problems: Carrot fly larvae tunnel into the roots.

CHARD / LEAF-BEET / SEAKALE BEET/ SPINACH BEET
Beta vulgaris cicla
Annual
Height 45cm (18in)
Excellent in large containers as well as beds
An attractive and delicious addition to any Urban Eden, this close relative of beetroot has generous leaves with marked midribs and veins. These range in colour from pale green or white through a stunning ruby-red variety and even yellow, pink, pink and white striped, orange and purple sold as 'rainbow chard'. The whole leaf, including the midrib, can be eaten, either together or separately, with the rib treated like asparagus.

Cultivation: Sow outdoors in spring in rich moisture-retentive soil for a summer harvest, sow in late summer for a late autumn one. Sow 3–4 seeds together, and thin when 10cm (4in) tall. Chard prefers soil that has been manured the season before planting.

Harvesting: A good cut-and-come-again crop. Cut outer leaves rather than pull them. Harvest regularly to ensure fresh growth.

CHILLIES
Capsicum spp
Height to 45cm (18in)
Good in containers
Chillies are very attractive plants with a neat, shrubby habit, lots of pretty, star-shaped flowers, then masses of fruit. Although tropical, because the plants mature quickly, they will fruit in temperate climates while the weather stays warm.

Apache produces masses of neat little chillies, and has a very attractive bushy shape; Chilli cayenne produces thin green fruit which turn red on ripening and is reliable even in temperate climates; Jalapeno is very hot, and prolific, but needs hot sun.

Cultivation: Start seeds indoors in the warmth, and grow on a sunny windowsill until summer is well established. The hotter the position, the happier the plant, and the hotter the pepper. Pick the fruit as they ripen.

At night, when it cools, chillies can look as though they are dying. Do not panic, they'll be fine next day.

COURGETTE
Cucurbita pepo
Annual
Height 45cm (18in), spreading to 1m² (3ft²)
Attractive in large containers
The courgette flower is attractively blowsy, fresh courgettes picked very small are delicious, and the plants make a generous

statement in late summer, covering a large area by the time they are mature. They are a useful addition in a border when many herbaceous plants are past their best. Choose from a range of different shapes and colours, from glossy dark-green cylindrical varieties such as Ambassador to the vivid golden-yellow Goldrush or even pale-green and white striped globes such as the romantically named Tondo Chiaro di Nizza.

Cultivation: Soak the seeds overnight, and sow indoors in spring, or directly into very well-manured soil after any risk of frost. Courgettes are greedy so feed and water well. They can cope with partial shade, but appreciate full sun and grow well in containers, tumbling over the side.

CUCUMBER
Cucumis sativus
Annual
Height 1.5m (5ft)
Good in windowboxes and containers
Ridge cucumbers produce a rough-skinned, spiny cucumber which is very crisp fresh off the vine. They like warmth but can be grown outdoors in cool, temperate climates if given protection in early stages. The bush varieties stay reasonably compact compared to the climbers which get up to 3m (10ft). Look for modern varieties which are self-fertile and have improved resistance to cold and disease. Kyoto is good grown up supports, with long thin fruit. Burpless Tasty Green crops well and freely. Bush champion also grows well in a container.

Cultivation: In late spring, germinate seeds indoors in a warm place such as an airing cupboard. Protect in pots until summer is under way, then plant out into very rich soil away from wind and direct sun, or into a sheltered windowbox. Grow up canes or wires, and pinch out the growing tip when there are 4–6 real leaves to encourage branching. Feed with high-potash fertiliser regularly to encourage fruiting.

Harvesting: Pick regularly to encourage continuous production of new fruit.

LEEKS
Allium ameloprasum
Annual
Height to 45cm (18in)
With their upright plume of grey-green architectural foliage, leeks are a good foil to other plants so excellent grown amongst other plants in borders or pots. They are very hardy and easy to grow in cooler climates, and if one or two are left in the bed rather than pulled, have attractive flowers. Musselburgh is very hardy with thick stems. King Richard makes a long plant and has a mild taste. Bleu de Solaise looks wonderful, the foilage has a bluish tinge, with a delightful taste, but the seeds are hard to get hold of.

Cultivation: Sow seeds indoors in spring, transplanting when 15–20cm (6–8in) high, or outside in summer. Make a hole for the seedlings 15cm (6in) deep, drop a plant into the hole and water well. This fills the hole with earth, which shouldn't be packed back. As the plant grows, earth up the stem to increase the length of blanched leek. You can pick them when they are no thicker than your thumb, or leave to grow bigger.

ONIONS
Allium cepa
Annual
Height to 45cm (18in)
It is difficult to grow onions from seed. Instead, buy onion sets. There is a great range to choose from, including strong-flavoured red-skinned varieties and torpedo-shaped varieties as well as the classic round brown-skinned onions. Choose varieties labelled bolt-resistant.

Cultivation: Onions will tolerate most soils as long as they have enough nutrients and some sun. The island of Lanzarote, where the soil is almost pure volcanic stone, grows quite wonderful onions. Though they prefer good soil, they dislike fresh manure, so manure the soil in early winter and plant sets in spring. If planting in a clump, place them at least 10cm (4in) apart. Sink the set into the soil so that only the nose is visible. Watering is only vital during a drought.

To encourage bulbs to grow feed with high-phosphate fertiliser (anything marketed as suitable for tomatoes) in summer, and pull back the earth from around the bulbs to let them ripen in the sun. At this stage they are very attractive. Harvest when the top bends over and the leaves begin to dry out. This is a sign that the goodness in the leaves has gone back into the bulb.

ORIENTAL GREENS
Brassica rapa var. chinensis
Annual
Height to 30cm (12in)
Good in troughs and beds
There are many different Oriental greens, most of which are superb for the Urban Eden, being compact, fast-growing annuals that respond well to cut-and-come-again treatment. They can be sown very late and early in the year, providing excellent winter salad or stir-fry greens, and grow well in beds, containers and windowboxes, providing late-season interest. Some of the most popular are Pak Choi, Mizuna and Mibuna.

Cultivation: Sow seed in rows in well-prepared fertile soil in a sunny or semi-shady position from March to October. Oriental greens prefer the cool and tend to bolt quickly in the heat. They are fast-growing, ready for harvesting within about 6 weeks of sowing – longer from late autumn or early spring sowings.

Harvesting: Use as cut-and-come-again; the first crop leaves are particularly full of flavour. The plant can be cut again twice or allowed to develop more, and cut about 3cm (1in) above ground, whereupon the stump will re-sprout.

Problems: Flea beetle can be a problem in spring sowings; the best solution is to cover your patch with a piece of horticultural fleece until seedlings are well established.

MANGETOUT PEAS / SUGARSNAP PEAS
Pisum sativum
Annual
Height to 60cm (2ft)
In a small space it is not worth growing maincrop peas unless they are particular favourites as they take up a lot of room and don't crop particularly heavily. But if you have the right conditions, mangetout are delicious and prolific.

Cultivation: Sow outside from mid-spring when the soil is warm. Peas prefer an open, sheltered position with a reasonably fertile, moisture-retentive, well-drained soil. They will not tolerate cold, drought, excessive heat or waterlogging.

Sow once early in the season, and again 6 weeks later for the best harvest.

Mangetout are a bit untidy and need support: either netting (which isn't attractive) or pea sticks, which are better. Like other legumes, the roots fix nitrogen, so when the plant has finished cropping, leave the roots in the soil to release their nitrogen into it.

POTATOES
Solanum tuberosum
Annual
Height to 1m (3ft)
Excellent in large containers
Since maincrop potatoes are always easily available in shops, and take up quite a lot of

space in a garden, it makes sense for the Urban Eden gardener to try early new potatoes, which produce wonderful, tasty potatoes best eaten absolutely fresh. They will grow very happily in deep containers. Rush them straight from the garden to boiling, salted water, and from there straight to the table. Delicious.

We have found good varieties for tubs are Rocket, Dunluce and the delicate early Swift. Try any early compact variety, or salad potatoes such as Blue Congo and Charlotte.

Cultivation: Plant sprouting seed potatoes in early March, 15cm (6in) deep in fertile soil. For the Urban Eden gardener, potatoes are excellent in a generous container at least 40cm (16in) deep which can be filled with soil-less compost for easiest cropping, as long as it is fed heavily with liquid feed and kept well watered, or in heavier soil-based compost enriched with manure.

Plant the potato half way down the pot and cover it with soil, and when the green shoot is about 30cm (12in) tall, cover it almost to the tip with earth to encourage more underground shoots to form. Some people stack two or three bottomless containers on top of each other and keep adding more earth to get a very generous crop.

Harvesting: Early-crop potatoes are ready when the flowers open. If you are careful, separate tubers can be pulled from the main root without disturbing the plant which will continue to produce more shoots and potatoes if it is kept well mounded up with earth. This is the potato equivalent of cut-and-come-again.

SHALLOTS

Allium ascalonicum
Annual
Height to 30cm (1ft)
Happy in containers and beds
Shallots are extemely easy to grow, and each bulb will produce a cluster of 8–10 bulbs. Buy heat-treated sets which have increased resistance to bolt.

Atlantic is a very heavy cropper with a fine flavour, and the attractive Golden gourmet produces a good number of smooth golden-yellow bulbs.

Cultivation: Plant sets in late winter or early spring. Shallots like a sheltered, sunny position and rich, moist, well-drained soil, but donít plant in newly manured earth. Make a small hole in the ground (better than pushing them in) sufficient to take the bulb but leave the tip just visible above the soil. Water during dry stretches. If you grow shallots in containers use soil-based compost with slow-release fertiliser added, and keep well watered in dry weather.

Shallots make good companions for apples and strawberry plants as they are believed to protect against fungus.

Harvesting: Harvest when leaves turn yellow. If dry, separate bulbs and leave on surface of soil for a week or so to dry out. If wet, dry indoors. Whilst drying, don't cut off green foliage as this can allow fungus infection into the bulb.

SPINACH

Spinacea oleracea
Annual
Height to 20cm (8in)
Good in containers and beds
An attractive leafy vegetable which is good for most Urban Edens, there are two main types of spinach, distinguished by seed. Round, smoot- seeded types cope well with high temperatures and are good for summer cropping, and prickly-seeded types are hardier and bolt in hot weather.

Cultivation: Seeds are traditionally soaked overnight to encourage germination and sown in spring directly into rich, moisture-retentive soil, in a bright but not too hot position. Spinach thrives in light shade. In frost-prone areas sow seed in pots of compost and transplant. You can sow several times a year for regular crops; a late summer sowing will produce a winter crop.

Spinach grows well in containers, but never let it dry out or it will bolt.

SWEETCORN

Zea mays
Annual
Height 1.5m (5ft)
A fantastic-looking plant, something like a large-leafed bamboo with leaves all the way up the stem. Because they are wind pollinated, it is best to grow them in blocks with plants about 30cm (12in) apart to maximise the chance that all the flowers set seed. They are not, however, the easiest of things to grow successfully as they are quite fussy in terms of weather, requiring sun, heat, a long growing season and regular water. If you were calculating production of food for space, they would not come top of the list as they only produce a couple of sweetcorns per plant. But they are very interesting, extremely ornamental, develop in a fascinating way, and fresh sweetcorn is much tastier than shop-bought sweetcorn. Early extra sweet matures fast and tolerates most climates.

Cultivation: The seeds and young plants hate cold soils so they should be sown inside and planted out in early summer. Sweetcorn grows on a wide range of soil as long as it is fertile and well drained (it will not tolerate waterlogging). Mulch the soil to help retain water.

Harvesting: The cobs are ripe when the tassels are droopy and milky juice comes from a corn when it is punctured.

The sugars in the corn start turning to starch within minutes of its being picked. So, if possible, have the water boiling on the cooker before you cut the cob. Get it into the water and cook it as soon as you cut it, and enjoy the taste sensation.

TOMATO
Lycopersicon esculentum
Annual
Height varies from 30cm (1ft) to 1.8m (6ft)
Excellent in containers and hanging baskets
Tomatoes grow well in beds and containers, crop freely and for a long time, with a fruit that is ornamental and very useful in the kitchen.

Cultivation: Sow seed in late spring with protection, or purchase small plants which are widely available. Plant out in early summer after all danger of frost has gone, and the soil is warm. Tomatoes prefer a sheltered, sunny position, and tolerate a wide range of soil as long as it is fertile and well drained. They are greedy feeders, requiring regular tomato fertiliser (high potash) to promote flowering and fruiting. Water well and regularly; tomatoes are thirsty too.

The larger tomatoes can be grown in the traditional way up canes, with side shoots pinched out, and the growing tip stopped when it has reached the desired height. But tomatoes can be grown loosely as a wall plant up trellis if you are interested in making the most of their quite attractive little yellow flowers.

Red Alert is a bush type with small, sweet fruit. Tumbler is a trailing variety which crops prolifically in hanging baskets and Gardener's Delight is a popular larger variety which has long trusses of small round fruit. Tigerella has fine-tasting red fruit that are flecked with pale stripes.

Harvesting: A ripe tomato parts from the stem when you lift it. Those that fall on the ground are super-ripe and make good sauce as long as you get to them before they rot. Although a few people might like green

tomato chutney, for most of us it is a lot of work, and then never gets eaten. Compost them instead.

Soft Fruit
There is a soft fruit plant for almost any space and almost any location, from the tiny alpine strawberry, through the standard gooseberry, to the potentially huge grapevine.

BLACKBERRIES
Rubus fruticosus
Most blackberries take up a significant amount of room, but they are very easy to grow, flower readily, and fruit even in the shade. So for some Urban Edens, they are a very useful plant.

Oregon Thornless is a beautiful plant, with fern-like leaves. It grows very well up a wall, but the fruit is not that tasty. Ashton Cross crops heavily, with fruit that tastes like wild blackberries.

Cultivation: Blackberries like rich soil but, provided the ground is not too dry, will tolerate poor soil. Although they flower and fruit even in cold, shady places, the fruit is sweeter in the sun. The fruited canes should be cut out each year after the berries have been picked.

BLACKCURRANTS
Ribes nigrum
When blackcurrants fruit, they look amazing, like a plant decorated with a host of black globes dangling on long pale stalks. For the rest of the season, they make a pleasant background for more exciting plants. Their foliage is also sharply aromatic.

Very hardy Ben Connan produces large well-flavoured berries. Ben Sarek is a small, compact grower with some mildew resistance. Baldwins has the best flavour.

Cultivation: Blackcurrants are greedy feeders so mulch well with plenty of well-rotted manure in spring to get a good crop. They prefer a sunny position, but will tolerate shade. They fruit on last year's growth, so after fruiting cut most of these old stems out and tie in the vigorous new growth which will then fruit well next year. Birds love blackcurrants, so you may have to protect canes with net or black cotton, and in dry climates mildew can be a problem.

BLUEBERRY
Vaccinium spp.
A very attractive shrub, with a delicious berry. Blueberries are partially self-fertile, but do better if two varieties are grown together.

Goldtraube is compact, a great cropper with good flavour. Bluecrop is early to mature, vigorous, with light-blue fruit with good flavour and very pretty autumn foliage.

Cultivation: Unless your garden is on acid soil, blueberries need to be cultivated in containers in ericaceous compost. They like moisture, and do best in sun. Use rainwater if possible when watering, particularly if your tapwater is alkaline. Blueberries do not need pruning: simply cut out dead wood in winter. If you want a compact bush, clip in spring.

Harvesting: The berries are ripe when they come off the bush easily.

GOOSEBERRY
Ribes uva crispa
Not an attractive shrub, but a lovely standard. Gooseberries can be grown in containers, but need a bit more care and attention than if grown in the ground.

Langley Gage is delicious and sweet. Pax Red is also disease-resistant.

Cultivation: Gooseberries prefer a good soil and some sun, and do not like hot, dry and sandy places. Also, as they are vulnerable to mildew, gooseberries do much better in breezy positions.

Pruning: Prune gooseberries back to juicy buds in winter if you want the bush to stay neat. Otherwise just ensure that the light and air can get to the centre of the bush.

Problems: Mildew is the big problem. This is exacerbated by still air, which is another argument in favour of standardising them so that the bush is above the stationary air of a bed.

GRAPE VINES
Vitis vinifera
Vines have interesting-looking leaves, beautiful fruit, and extraordinary bark that gets increasingly characterful as they age. In temperate climates, the fruit is usually not very sweet, but it is exciting to watch them attempt to ripen.

Boskoop Glory is a delicious dark grape, hardy and reliable. Regent is a new outdoor dessert red which is resistant to mildew and downy mildew. Leon Millet is a black dessert grape with good mildew resistance.

Cultivation: Vines are greedy feeders that develop deep roots and are difficult to grow in containers. They like warm weather, a sunny wall, and superbly drained soil. For good-sized grapes, mulch vines in spring with manure. They also appreciate regular feeding in summer.

Pruning: Vines are fast-growing and, left unpruned, will produce a vast amount of foliage and tendrils. They fruit on current season's growth, and with a lot of growth will bear far too many bunches of grapes which will be tiny. All the pruning and training systems – and there are many of them – are designed to keep these impulses in check.

The principles are to allow a maximum of four stems to grow from the rootstock. Cut back all main stems by two thirds in autumn each year to establish a framework of older wood. The laterals from these main branches should be allowed to grow only about 50cm (20in). When the vine flowers, cut off all the branch beyond the clusters of flowers, leaving only a leaf or two. This puts the energy of the vine into the bunch, and helps the air and sun get to the fruit. If you want good-sized grapes, keep only one bunch per lateral. Prune any other shoots on these laterals back to one leaf. Prune back non-flowering laterals to about five leaves.

Once the framework of the vine is established, in winter cut the main stems back to two strong buds on the framework, and the laterals to one strong bud.

Harvesting: As the bunches swell, remove any berries that are misshapen or diseased. In warmer climates, where dessert grapes can be grown, thin the bunch to allow the remaining berries to swell. Remove any leaves around the bunches to help sun get to the fruit.

Problems: In spite of their vigour, vines are delicate. The fruit on older varieties goes mouldy during moist seasons, and the leaves get mildew in the dry.

Vine weevils, as their name suggest, particularly like vines (see page 110).

RASPBERRIES
Rubus idaeas
Because a raspberry is not actually a very attractive plant, grow them only if you love the taste of them, as home-grown, fresh-picked raspberries are far superior to the tasteless berries sold in shops.

Autumn Bliss is autumn-fruiting and can be picked late into the growing season, so this is a very useful late crop. Glen Ample fruits in mid-season, with prolific, large, fleshy fruit.

Cultivation: Raspberries will tolerate fairly heavy shade, and actually prefer cool, moist conditions, with rich moisture-retentive soil. Be careful when growing them against walls to provide enough moisture.

Pruning: Pruning is easy. With raspberries that fruit in autumn, cut all the canes to the ground in late winter. Summer-fruiting raspberries fruit on the previous year's growth so cut the fruit-bearing canes to the ground after fruiting and tie the new growth onto a framework to bear fruit the next year.

Problems: Birds love raspberries, so swathe them in black cotton or netting.

STRAWBERRIES
Fragaria
Put crudely, there are two kinds of strawberries: the wild, alpine strawberries *Fragaria vesca semperflorens* and the cultivated, modern hybrids. Alpine strawberries produce a lovely little heart-shaped fruit that is tangy and scented, but not very sweet and juicy over most of the summer; and the hybrids produce much bigger, glossier fruit which are much sweeter and juicier. The alpines are probably better suited to growing in the ground in the Urban Eden as they are tough, flower for a long period, and produce fruit that is very different from the strawberries available in the shops. The hybrids are better in containers, as they require more care.

There are lots of good hybrids but a few to look out for are Aromel with its long fruiting period (described as 'perpetual') and a good flavour. Cambridge Favourite is reliable, tolerant of a range of conditions and easy to grow. Cambridge Late Pine has excellent flavour.

Cultivation: Alpine strawberries are grown from seed. Plant in the bed when big enough to handle. They prefer moist, partial shade and rich soil, but can be grown very successfully in hanging baskets, well away from the slugs that adore them at ground level. Buy hybrids as plants (or runners). They prefer a very rich soil full of organic matter, and full sun. If you wish to keep the plants after fruiting, cut off all the leaves to within 10cm (4in) of the crown. After three years get rid of the old plants and raise new ones, in fresh compost, from runners.

Problems: Hybrids are more difficult than Alpines. Their fruit will rot if there is too much moisture, so need to be protected (by straw if they are grown in the soil, hence the name). Birds also love them.

Tree Fruit

Fruiting trees are very dependent on the yearly cycle of weather. In many years it works: the flowers are fertilised by the bees, there is enough rain and enough sun. Other years, it just doesn't: it might be a late frost, or too little rain, or too much wind. The important thing to realise is that even without a fabulous fruit crop, fruit trees look good and provide lots of interest. And there is always next year.

What follows is once again a selection of plants that are particularly suited to a small urban garden. They are plants which fruit fairly reliably and don't require an enormous input of time. The interesting thing about fruit is that many Urban Eden gardeners don't even actually eat what their trees bear, but enjoy the rollercoaster ride, and watching the birds take most of it.

Most fruit trees are sold as container-grown plants, as these can be sold and planted out at any time of year. By the end of the season, however, many of these trees will be a little pot-bound. This is something to watch out for with container-grown trees, which develop an unnatural fibrous root system. To do well with container-grown

trees, tease out the roots to encourage them to spread when they are planted out.

If you want to do something more complicated with a fruit tree than just grow it as a bush – such as create a fruit arch – buy a bare-rooted tree direct from a nursery in autumn or winter. Although when these arrive they will appear to have little root, what is there is stronger and more natural than the roots of container-grown plants, and the trees often grow better when planted out.

Fruit grows very well in containers as long as it is on the right rootstock. As this is a permanent planting, refresh the soil regularly with a good dressing of manure and compost.

For a guide to planting fruit trees, see Chapter 6, Winter, p126.

APPLES

Malus domestica

Producing wonderful pink and white blossom in spring, apple trees fruit quickly after planting and are great for small gardens. So many varieties have such value that it is difficult to select particular ones, but here are some thoughts.

Falstaff Red is self-fertile, frost-resistant, fruits in the first year with a good flavour. Red Devil has a great flavour, is disease-resistant and very easy to grow. Princesse is a russet type, a heavy cropper. Blenheim Orange can be used both as a cooker and an eater and ripens well even in poor summers. Red Windsor is rather like a compact cox but is disease-resistant.

Cox is a superb-tasting apple but a difficult tree to grow, prone to disease, and preferring a reliably warm summer. Only grow if prepared to struggle with it.

Bramley is a 'triploid', meaning it requires two other varieties for pollination and subsequent fruiting. Only advisable for those who are planting a mini-orchard, or whose garden is surrounded by other apple trees.

Ballerina apples are dwarf and trees grow as columns. The fruit generally tastes poor.

Family apple trees are a great idea in principle, especially for a very small garden for those keen on home-grown apples. Three varieties are grafted onto one rootstock, chosen so they pollinate one another. This ensures that the tree crops. However, in practice, family trees look distinctly weird, and can grow in a very unbalanced way.

Rootstocks: In common with many other fruit trees, most apples are grafted onto rootstocks that maintain the mature tree at a certain size. So when buying an apple, check the rootstock. These are some of the commoner dwarf rootstocks.

M27: Very dwarf, ideal for very small gardens or a pot.

MM106: Medium-sized, grows well on poorer soil and is probably the most suitable for most small gardens.

M26: Semi-dwarf, so in theory good for small gardens. But the trunk on this rootstock is often weak so needs staking.

M9: Dwarf, but needs staking.

PIXIE is very dwarf, often used for varieties specially designed for container growing.

Pollination: Few apples are self-fertile, but since eating apples are also pollinated by crab apples (Malus Golden Hornet, Everest and Golden Gem amongst others), a garden surrounded by other gardens is likely to contain something that will fertilise an apple. But to be sure of pollination, plant an apple pollinator along with the apple. Nurseries and garden centres always stock plenty of these.

Cultivation: Apples can grow in most soils but they prefer a well-drained soil which at the same time holds water well. It's the usual refrain: plenty of organic matter is needed. They will not tolerate being waterlogged. Never plant a new apple tree in the same spot where an old one has been taken out.

Problems: Apples tend to suffer from many pests and diseases, but seem usually to fruit pretty well anyway. Pruning the tree so that it is open helps (see Chapter 3), and selecting a new variety marketed as disease-resistant will also mean you have to spend less time and effort keeping your crop clean.

CHERRY
Prunus spp.

A beautiful tree in flower and fruit, but not very attractive in winter. Stella is very reliable, self-fertile, with large juicy fruit. Celeste is a new variety, compact, self-fertile, with excellent flavour. Sylvia is very dwarf, with very good fruit. Morello is a cooking cherry, the very best fruit tree for shady or north walls, less attractive in flower than most cherries, but with delicious tart fruit.

Cultivation: Cherries need good soil that contains lots of organic matter. For small gardens, a plant grafted onto a semi-dwarf rootstock is a must. 'Colt' is a good semi-dwarf; 'Tabel' is a full dwarf. Cherries do not need pruning, but cut out any diseased growth to encourage an open structure in the spring.

Problems: Bacterial canker can kill a tree. Cherries are also prone to weather-related diseases. To deter birds, throw black cotton over the tree. The silhouette of a raptor hung over the tree also helps.

FIG
Ficus carica

One of the world's oldest cultivated fruits, figs are wonderful in large pots or as large shrubs, though they need the protection of a warm wall in cooler areas.

They fruit willingly, though in bad summers the fruits may not ripen. Fig trees have a subtle aroma when in full sun, and stunning large cut leaves.

In Mediterranean climates you can choose between a dozen or so good varieties, but in cooler temperate climates the most reliable outdoor varieties are Brown Turkey, Brunswick and White Marseilles, which has pale-green fruit.

Cultivation: Plant in well-drained and well-manured soil with an inch of the stem under the ground to protect the roots from frost. For heavy cropping, restrict the roots by lining the hole with paving slabs or planting in a large, deep, submerged container. Too much watering as the figs ripen may cause the fruits to split. In containers use free-draining loam-based compost, and protect the pot with straw, sacking or bubblewrap in cold winters.

Remove any unripe figs in the autumn, and feed the tree with high-potash feeds in the summer.

Picking: Pick fruit in late summer when they start to droop and soften. Eat as soon as possible as they deteriorate quickly unless dried.

GREENGAGES
Prunus italica

Ripe greengages are fabulous, more honeyed than plums. But since they don't handle well, they are increasingly difficult to buy. The greengages that are picked green and hard never ripen properly.

If for no other reason than that they are delicious, they are worth growing. The tree stays quite small if grafted onto Pixie rootstock and flowers are attractive although short-lasting.

Self-fertile and shade-tolerant Oulins Golden Gage bears golden-yellow fruit with the typical greengage honeyed taste. Dennistons Superb is a very reliable, self-fertile heavy cropper but the taste is rather bland. Willingham Gage has excellent flavour, is self-fertile and a heavy cropper.

Cultivation: Greengages like well-drained, fertile soil. In cooler areas they require some shelter, but can crop reasonably even on a north-facing wall.

Problems: Greengages crop irregularly. When they do bear, birds seek them out as they are so sweet. Protect with black cotton. In a good summer, when there is a heavy crop, wasps can become a problem. Wasp traps may be needed (put some sugary water in a jam jar. Cover with foil, pierced with holes big enough for a wasp to squeeze into. Hang from the tree near the fruit).

MEDLAR
Mespilus germanica

Medlar trees are beautiful, they bear lovely single white flowers with a golden centre in spring, have good autumn colours and delicious fruit. The only thing that stops a medlar being the perfect fruit tree for the Urban Eden is that the fruit needs to be 'bletted' and is a distinctly acquired taste, being mushy and custardy.

The best-tasting medlar is Nottingham, a compact tree with medium-sized fruit.

Cultivation: Medlars are easy-going, growing in most conditions as long as they are not waterlogged. They like to grow in lawns.

Harvesting: Leave the fruit on the tree until they part easily when lifted. Pick on a dry day. To blet the fruit, store in a dry, cool place. After 2–3 weeks the outside will be wrinkly, and the flesh will be soft and brown. This is the time to eat it.

PEACHES
Prunus persica

A peach is a great tree for a small garden. It has pretty pink blossom in spring, and supremely delicious fruit. But peaches are fussy, and peach leaf curl, which is borne in the rain, can make the tree look leprous.

Duke of York has excellent taste and fruit ripens early. Peregrine is probably the best peach for cooler climates, ripening in mid-August with yellow-fleshed fruit with excellent flavour. Lord Napier is a reasonably hardy nectarine suitable for outdoor cultivation in warmer climates.

Cultivation: Plant peaches against a sunny wall in well-enriched soil that is not clayey. Good drainage is vital. The trees grow well in a lawn as grass actually helps to conserve potash in the soil which peaches appreciate. Once established, a peach tree needs less water than other fruit because its roots go surprisingly deep. They prefer a slightly alkaline soil, so it pays to add chalk to soil that is acid.

Peaches fruit on new growth so to contain a tree, cut out the branches that have held fruit to encourage new growth from low down. It is common to train peaches onto walls as a fan. Tie in new growth to replace old branches once they have fruited.

Harvesting: Wait until the fruit smells good before harvesting.

Problems: Peach leaf curl is a fungal disease. The spores are carried in raindrops, and invade the leaf buds as they fatten in spring. A peach with leaf curl looks pathetic, and won't fruit properly if at all. There is no way to cure it once a leaf is hit. Remove infected leaves and the new ones may come back straight.

There are two methods of prevention. One is to provide the tree with a polythene cover as the buds swell to keep the rain off. Be careful to tuck the polythene under to keep rain (and spores) from splashing off the soil onto the plant. This can be removed once the new leaves appear. The second method is to spray with Bordeaux mixture twice as the buds start to swell. In autumn, pick up all old leaves and burn them.

PEARS
Pyrus communis
When mature, a pear tree is majestic. The flowers are glorious, the shape of the tree is classical, and the bark is deeply cut and very attractive.

Doyenne du Comice produces heavy crops of sweet, juicy fruit. Beth is a good choice for small gardens, a compact tree producing small, very sweet and juicy fruit. Concorde is also very compact, is self-fertile and crops heavily.

Cultivation: Pears prefer a deep rich soil, but will grow pretty well anywhere. Although they work surprisingly well in pots, they can look a bit out of proportion.

Harvesting: The pear is ripe when it naturally parts from the tree.

Problems: Because pears flower early in the season, they are vulnerable to late frosts. In colder areas, plant a pear tree near a wall. Pears suffer from fewer pests and diseases than apples, but are more affected by the weather. A late frost will destroy the crop; a cool summer will mean hard pears.

PLUMS
Prunus domestica
Plum trees bear beautiful blossom, and lovely fruit, but look slightly gloomy in winter.

Victoria is self-fertile, good in shade, prolific and fruits have superb flavour, but the trees are prone to disease. Jubileum is more disease-resistant, producing equally delicious large fruit.

Cultivation: Plums like quite heavy soils, so will tolerate quite a lot of clay. Plums grown on Pixie rootstock stay dwarf, but – unusually – this affects the size of the fruit too.

Problems: Plums blossom early, so are susceptible to spring frosts.

Even though plums are subject to a lot of diseases and pests, as long as the fruit sets (which depends on the weather at the time they fruit being warm enough for bees to be active) they usually fruit well.

QUINCE
Cydonia vulgaris
A delightful tree, quince flowers are large, creamy and soft, the fruit is beautiful and fragrant, and the autumn colours are delightfully bright. When cooked, quinces make superb jams, purées and preserves (see Recipes, p 141).

Vranja is self-fertile, producing large well-flavoured fruit on an erect tree. Portuguese bears vigorous crops of pear-shaped fruit, but takes a few years to crop. Meaches Prolific is also self-fertile with attractive bright-yellow fruit when ripe.

Cultivation: Quinces prefer warm, moist conditions. They have no particular soil requirements and even seem to grow well on heavy clay soils. Quinces can grow quite happily in large containers in fairly rich soil.

The flowers appear quite early in spring and a late frost can destroy the fruit. Prune in winter to remove crossing wood and to allow light and air into the tree.

Harvesting: Pick in autumn when the fruit is fully formed.

index

acknowledgements

The authors would like to thank David Kerley, Nick Dunn and Ken Black for their horticultural advice; Kate Davies, Senior Lecturer, Bath Spa University College, for her lucid explanation of the effects of lead from car exhausts on soil; Dr Chris Turner for his help on soils; Bob Gilbert for generously sharing with us his knowledge of the wildlife to be found in the urban environment; Penelope Bennet, Xa Tollemache, Roy Balaam, Nick, Bunny and Max McMahon, Maddy Fisk, Helen Pitel, Gavin Jones,* John Leslie,** Glynis Murray, Henry Braham and our father for letting us see and in some cases photograph their great gardens; Joe Swift and Stephanie Donaldson for help and support when we most needed it; Francesca Yorke for her wonderful photographs and her assistant Sam; Gilly Love for the styling; Charlie Ryrie for her expertise and guidance in all matters horticultural; Vanessa Courtier for her inspiring design work and Gina Hochstein for the scanning and typesetting; and Kate Oldfield, Sheila Boniface and all the team at Kyle Cathie who have managed us with patience and helped us produce a book we are very proud of.

All photography by Francesca Yorke, except for the following: Nicola Browne p 18 & 19; Eric Crichton (Garden Picture Library) p75; Robert Estall (GPL) p107; Vaughan Fleming (GPL) p103; John Glover (GPL) pp61, 64, 67 & 72; Georgia Glynn-Smith (GPL) p81; Sunniva Harte (GPL) p73; A.I.Lord (GPL) p70; John Miller (GPL) p69; Camille Muller (GPL) p69; Derek St. Romaine pp65 & 75; Mel Watson (GPL) pp39 & 81 and Steven Wooster (GPL) p75.

*pp 85-7. Gavin Jones started his practice Jones Environmental in 1997 based on the work at Cameron Gardens. At the forefront of 'Bell jar ecology' he specialises in designing urban community gardens and modular ecological building systems. Visit his website at: www.ecospires.com
**pp 71 (left), 77 (bottom) and 80. Designed and planted by John Leslie Gardens. Visit his website at: www.johnlesliegardens.co.uk

First published in Great Britain in 2000 by Kyle Cathie Limited, 122 Arlington Road, London NW1 7HP

ISBN 1 85626 350 9

Editor Kate Oldfield **Copy Editor** Morag Lyall **Editorial Assistant** Sheila Boniface **Designer** Vanessa Courtier **Design Assistant** Gina Hochstein **Stylist** Gilly Love **Home Economist** Emma Patmore

A CIP catalogue record for this title is available from the British Library

Printed and bound in Toledo, Spain by Artes Graficas
D.L. TO: 1825 - 1999